# CREATIVE LIVING
## from
# ORIGINAL DESIGN

**Betsy Fritcha**

ISBN 978-1-0980-8039-6 (paperback)
ISBN 978-1-0980-8040-2 (digital)

Copyright © 2021 by Betsy Fritcha

All rights reserved. No part of this publication may be reproduced, distributed, or transmitted in any form or by any means, including photocopying, recording, or other electronic or mechanical methods without the prior written permission of the publisher. For permission requests, solicit the publisher via the address below.

Christian Faith Publishing, Inc.
832 Park Avenue
Meadville, PA 16335
www.christianfaithpublishing.com

Printed in the United States of America

# Contents

## The Immeasurable Holy Operations of
**Supreme God** ........................................................... 28
Disruption of the Earth ............................................. 28
God Is Working in Unseen Ways ............................. 30
Partaking in God's Glory Being Revealed ................ 31
Halting Old Methods ................................................. 32
Bringing in New Ways .............................................. 33
Written in God's Books ............................................. 35

## Manifest Glory Operations ................................. 36
Molecular Restructure .............................................. 37
Greater Works ........................................................... 39
Gabriel Brings Visionary Glory Box ......................... 41
Invisible Substance of Life—Material Manifestation ..... 46
Invisible Atoms, DNA, and Transmuted RNA .......... 52
Drawing on God's Glory Substance ......................... 55
Gabriel Brings Glory Fire Messages ........................ 55
The Council of the Godly .......................................... 58
What Do Angels Know .............................................. 61
Procreating by Perverted Angels ............................. 61
Legitimate Holy Procreating .................................... 62
Thoughts Are Doings ................................................ 65
God's Mesh of Communication Wires ..................... 68

## Creative Glory Acts ............................................... 69
Personal Holy Supernatural Encounters ................. 72
Holy Spirit Adventures ............................................. 75
Personal Supernatural Encounter ........................... 77
Steering Wheels—Magnetic Force ........................... 79
Pure Worship Creates Glory Substance .................. 82
Transporting Visionary Glory .................................. 85
Unused Words in Visionary Glory Box .................... 86

Religious Spirit and Human Will Join ........................ 87
Religious Spirit Rendered Powerless ....................... 92
Church Leaders and Religious Spirit ........................ 96
Satan Rendered Powerless ....................................... 98

**Time to Construct and Create** ........................... 102
Unlocking Supernatural Provision ........................... 106
Supernatural Acts Defy World's Logic ..................... 108
Kingdom Shift Back to Original Design .................... 109
Overseers in Charge of Cities ................................ 117

The cover design for this book, *Creative Living from Original Design,* is the creative design of my high school granddaughter Elleysn Fritcha.

Elle has won numerous creative-art awards. Her artwork is displayed in various places around our city. Elle has been publicly acknowledged for her artwork, athletic, and academic accomplishments through our local newspaper, the Fort Wayne *Journal Gazette,* and on Fort Wayne WANE-TV sports reports.

She was asked by her high school to paint a whole mural depicting people's ideas they gave her. She created their ideas through inspiration and painted them freehand. This has gained her widespread honor. Her artwork is also displayed in various places in and around her home city.

Elle recently graduated from high school and is now in college. She continues to exemplify Holy God's creative ability that He innately designed in her that display His creative nature. Elle has been asked by her college to use her artistic skills to enhance their college campus and the surrounding area and to assist her college's marketing team.

# Creative Living from Original Design

I have intentionally written *Creative Living from Original Design* conforming to no literary protocol, which I adhered to in all the other books that I have had published.

**What is written in this book is raw Truth for anyone who cares to rightly analyze Wisdom in order to Creatively achieve their Eternal Destiny.**

So here goes!

Have you ever desired to live in an environment that was as perfect as you imagined it to be? A reality place where you could just be you? A place where you were free to create anything you could think of and for it to remain and even creatively expand just the way you desire and envision? Have you ever tried to create an environment for yourself and your loved ones as you wanted it to be only to have others' self-imposed ways forced upon you obligating you to conform to their way of thinking?

Do you truly have a strong desire to build and create something that is innately in you that you cannot seem to dismiss or erase?

Have you ever considered what it would be like to live in an environment free from opposition?

What if this were possible? Would you seek to know how this could actually be accomplished?

Well, I have good news for you. This is possible. Creator God Planned for you to live in Perfect Harmony and Creativity for Infinity.

Every human being is Created in the Image and Likeness of a Creatively Unique GOD who formed within each person a definite designed pattern of creativity so that each person can form inventive ways to expand their lives that only they can complete for their personal enjoyment.

Creative God's *Will* for Creating humankind in His exact Image and Likeness is for His personal enjoyment of watching His Created people creatively create their own environment for Good purposes. He wants His Created human beings to mirror His Creative Ability He innately placed in them that is good and benefits them and others as well. He is not a selfish God. He shares His Creative Ability with people He Designed to be like Himself. Therefore, He wants to come alongside you and be part of your life. He deeply desires that you create the environment you envision from the original design He innately placed within you before you ever born.

I write this book using my God-given and unique creative abilities to write what He designed in me to accomplish. My desire is to enhance your creative ability so you can learn how to creatively design and accomplish your Infinite destiny He Planned for you to accomplish.

Creative God's Original Plan included creating humankind in His very own Image and after His Likeness for His Infinite Purpose to have someone like Himself who can create the environment they want to inhabit in the same way He does. God enjoys sharing His Creative Ability with you. Watching you creatively accomplish your personal desires and intents for good that He placed in you brings Him everlasting Enjoyment.

You must know and understand, however, that there are sinister operations irrationally endeavoring to remove human beings from fulfilling their innately-designed destiny. Consider rationally that one of these sinister operations is to remove human being's gender identity.

Is anyone asking why there is rampant perversion of sexual identity on earth today? Why are people cynically being pushed into deciding what gender they want to be?

Perverted culture is telling people that they can choose their gender by electing to transgender from their born gender, and even declare they are nongender. Hogwash! Creative God created you to be the gender He wanted you to be. There is beauty and creativity in being male or female. Each gender needs the other and cannot be complete without the other's involvement. Just logically think this through! If there were neither male nor female genders, you wouldn't be here.

If evil intent can remove humankind's gender uniqueness as either male or a female, they can no longer reproduce and have dominion of the earth to create their environment for good. Therefore, manipulative operations are being used through cultural savvy to convince humankind to become nongender, which is totally ludicrous.

This sinister ploy of removing gender identity is to prevent humankind from achieving their innate creative ability to procreate their environment as they so choose. This threatening operation if allowed to be accomplished by human neglect has the ability to stop humankind from creating a personally designed environment that suits their God-designed destiny. If humankind accepts this perverted plan, Creative God's intended destiny for them to create their environment for good purposes is thwarted and eventually shut down.

Along with this heinous maneuver, those who cannot be convinced to become nongender or transgender are being duped into aborting their creatively conceived babies in the womb of their mothers. Each person's creative identity was planned by an Infinite Creator before they were ever born into this world, and each has an innate destiny to fulfill.

Therefore, no matter how it seems or appears to be, nothing can stop these Created babies from fulfilling their predetermined Infinite destinies planned for them by Creative God. Sinister operations can never stop the created destinies of these aborted babies from being fulfilled. They immediately go into the Presence of their Heavenly Father and continue their created destinies. The Holy Bible states truth:

*Jesus called a little child to his side and said to his disciples, "Learn this well: Unless you dramatically change your way of thinking and become teachable, and learn about heaven's kingdom realm with the wide-eyed wonder of a child, you will never be able to enter in. Whoever continually humbles himself to become like this gentle child is the greatest on in heaven's kingdom realm. And if you tenderly care for this little one on my behalf, you are tenderly caring for me. But if anyone abuses one of these little ones who believe in me, it would be better for him to have a heavy boulder tied around his neck and be hurled in the deepest sea than to face the punishment he deserves."*

CREATIVE LIVING FROM ORIGINAL DESIGN

*Be careful that you not corrupt one of these little ones. For I can assure you that I heaven each of their angelic guardians have instant access to my heavenly Father.* (Matthew 18:1-6, 10)

*Jesus said to his disciples who were indignant that little children were bring brought to him; and he said to them, "I want little children to come to me, so never interfere with them when they want to come, for heaven's kingdom realm is composed of beloved ones like these! Listen to the truth: No one will enter the kingdom realm of heaven unless he becomes like one of these."* (Matthew 19:13-15)

*Good people pass away; the godly often die before their time. But no one seems to care or wonder why. No one seems to understand that God is protecting them from the evil to come. Those who follow godly paths will rest in peace when they die.* (Isaiah 57:1-2 NLT)

Illogical and sinister operations deriving from a perverted being, namely the devil or Satan, presume that if humankind accepts perverted and evil logic, they can no longer multiply and creatively create their infinite destines as Creative God mandated them to do. Read in The Holy Bible Genesis 1:26-28, Psalm 8, Isaiah 65:17-25, Hebrews 1-2.

Blatant evil plots are being overtly spread with the intent of shutting down human beings from creatively creating their own environment as God Designed them to do. These evil plots also interrupt people from joining with other people's creativity for their shared enjoyment.

The devil cannot reproduce after his kind. He has to transform himself into a human being and present himself as a viable partner to cohabit with sexually. Any willing human woman who allows herself to illegally cohabit with him reproduces corrupted freaks who disrupt society. His perverted plan is to illegally fabricate a people and kingdom he can rule over.

This sinister and evil intent of removing gender identity is pretty stupid if you think about it with intelligence. If there are no longer human beings procreating to govern the earth as Creative God skillfully Designed them to do, eventually there will be no one left for him to cohabit with in making freaks, so therefore, he will have no one left to rule an illicit and perverted kingdom of his irrationally imagined intent. Why would you want to conform to being a freak when you can creatively create and design your own environment for good as Creative God designed for you to accomplish for your personal enjoyment?

Yes, there is an evil devil whose intended purpose is totally wicked. He never relents in attempting to take creatively designed human beings away from their Creator's Good Plan for them. Each person needs to consider that when humankind creatively designs and creates their environment for good to enjoy both now and for Infinity, evil and sinister operations are closed down permanently.

The devil never relents in attempting to corrupt human beings by lies and deception to gain power control over them so he can rule them by intimidation and fear. Will you allow yourself to be illicitly used for the devil's illegal plans which eventually destroys you forever and ever stopping the creative ability you have been given by Creative God? Each person has to personally answer this question and as well give an account to their Creator as to why they chose evil over Good.

Supreme God of Heaven and earth Creatively Designed each human being with unique abilities to creatively design and create the environment in which they wish to live and enjoy for Infinity. He wants each person to know from His Heart of Love and Truth that you were Created by Him to live in Joy and Peace and Creativity in perfect harmony with Him and other people for ever and ever with no end.

Holy God's *Will* was established before He Created anything and before the world began. His Holy Plan can never be changed or permanently thwarted. He has sworn by Himself that His *Will* is True and established forever. He upholds His Name and His Word Eternally over all Creation. *The promises of Your Word are backed up by the honor or Your Name* (Psalms 138:2).

Therefore, God of Love, Truth, and Wisdom asked me to publish His Creatively Designed Intent which is for humankind to know how to uniquely create and design their Eternal Destiny He intends for them to realize and accomplish. He is willingly and visibly revealing His Holy Plan for all who truthfully want to learn how to implement His Original Holy Intent for each person He Created in His Image and Likeness. These are Holy ways of living that perpetuate and expand throughout Eternity.

This book, *Creative Living from Original Design*, entails Holy encounters producing divine revelations. Holy God is Sovereignly revealing how you can factually *train* yourself to Creatively live from Original Design both now and for Infinity. Creative God wrote down in The Holy Bible His instructions for Eternal Living according to His Original Designed Intent. From Genesis to Revelation God lays out His Plan for Eternal Living.

He as well has innately designed into each person their Eternal destiny.

*For You formed my inward parts. You covered me in my mother's womb. I will praise You, for I am fearfully and wonderfully made. Marvelous are Your works, and that my soul knows very well. My frame was not hidden from You. When I was made in secret, and skillfully wrought in the lowest parts of the earth Your eyes saw my substance yet unformed, and in Your book they all were written. The days fashioned for me, when as yet there were none of them." (Psalms 139:13-16)*

Therefore, redeemed humankind can frame The Father's Words and speak them forth into visible manifestation from their intrinsically Designed intent that is innately within them.

Holy God's time has come to openly reveal, to those who obey His directions, how they are to fulfill His Creative Design for them as documented in The Holy Bible.

*Says The Lord, "So shall My Word be that goes forth from My mouth. It shall not return to Me void or empty of fulfillment. But it shall accomplish what I please, and it shall prosper in the thing for which I sent it.* **(**Isaiah 55:11)

*In the beginning was the Word, and the Word was with God and the Word was God. He was in the beginning with God. All things were made through Him, and without Him nothing was made that was made. In Him was* (and is) *Life, and the Life was* (and is) *the Light of men. And the Light shines in the darkness, and the darkness did not comprehend it. (John 1:1-5)*

*...the Word became flesh and dwelt among us, and we beheld His Glory, the Glory as of the only begotten of the Father, full of Grace and Truth.* (John 1:14)

*If you abide in Me [Jesus Christ, The Word of God made flesh, sent to earth by His Father to speak only those things the Father gave Him to speak—John 8:28-29] and My words abide in you, you will ask what you desire, and it shall be done for you.* (John 15:7)

*The Spirit of Truth has come, He will guide you into all Truth; for He will not speak on His own Authority, but whatever He hears He will speak; and He will tell you things to come. He will Glorify Me, for He will take of what is Mine and declare it to you. All things that the Father has are Mine; therefore, I said that He will take of Mine and declare it to you.* (John 16:13-15)

*Jesus Christ is the same yesterday, today, and forever.* (Hebrews 13:8)

*Your Father in Heaven is speaking Truth to those who choose to believe and seek Truth from the Words He continuously speaks to them.*

*But God speaks again and again, though people do not recognize it. He speaks in dreams, in visions of the night when deep sleep falls on people as they lie in bed. He whispers in their ear and terrifies them with His warning. He causes them to change their minds; He keeps them from pride. He keeps them from the grave, from crossing over the river of death. Or God disciplines people with sickness and pain, with ceaseless aching in their bones. They lose their appetite and do not care for even the most delicious food. They waste away to skin and bones. They are at death's door; the angels of death wait for them.*

*But if a special messenger from Heaven is there to intercede for a person, to declare that He is upright, God will be gracious and say, 'Set him free. Do not make him die for I have found a ransom for his life.' Then his body will become as healthy as a child's, firm and youthful again. When he prays to God, he will be accepted. And God will receive him with joy and restore him to good standing. He will declare to his friends, 'I sinned, but it was not worth it. God rescued me from the grave, and now my life is filled with light.'*

*Yes, God often does these things for people He rescues them from the grave so they may live in the Light of the living."* (Job 33:14-29)

For those who freely choose to truly believe, trust, and obey The Word of God who is Jesus the Son of God who came in human flesh to do His Father's *Will* the recorded Word of God is still being written because Holy Spirit is continuously speaking The Father and Jesus' Word of Truth into the earth through those who believe the Word of The Father and His Son, Jesus, and so speak their Words of Truth into existence.

*And there are also many other things that Jesus did, which if they were written one by one, I suppose that even the world itself could not contain the books that would be written. Amen.* (John 21:25)

These things that Jesus came on earth in human flesh to show us how to do are still being performed and recorded in the Books in Heaven. These things continue for Infinity through us who ask The Father in Jesus' Name.

Jesus says:
*You did not choose Me, but I chose you and appointed you that you should go and bear fruit, and that your fruit should remain, and whatever you ask the Father in My Name He may give you. (John 15:16)*

*If you abide in Me, and My Words abide in you, ask whatever you will, and it shall be done for you. (John 15:7)*

*Ask and it will be given you; seek, and you will find; knock, and it will be opened to you. For everyone who asks receives, and he who seeks finds, and to him who knocks it will be opened. (Matthew 7:7-8)*

*Have faith in God. Truly, I say to you, whoever says to this mountain, 'Be taken up and cast into the sea,' and does not doubt in his heart, but believes that what he says will come to pass, it will be done for him. Therefore, I tell you, whatever you ask in prayer, believe that you receive it, and you will. And whenever you stand praying, believe that you have received it, and you will. And whenever you stand praying, forgive, if you have anything against anyone; so that your Father who is in Heaven may also forgive your trespasses. (Mark 11:22-26)*

*For if you forgive men their trespasses, your heavenly Father will also forgive you; but if you do not forgive men their trespasses from your heart, neither will your Father forgive you. (Matthew 6:14-15)*

*Truly, truly, I say to you, he who believes in Me will also do the works that I do; and greater works than these will he do, because I go to the Father. Whatever you ask in My Name, I will do it, that the Father may be glorified in the Son; if you ask anything in My Name, I will do it. (John 14:12-14)*

*I (Jesus) have spoken these things to you while I was with you. The Counselor, Holy Spirit, whom the Father will send in My Name, He will teach you all things, and bring to your remembrance all that I have said to you.* (John 14:25-26)

*I, Paul (and all of us who are in Christ Jesus) who am a fellow elder and a witness of the sufferings of Christ, and also* **a partaker of the glory that will be revealed**... (1 Peter 5:1)

What is written in this book, *Creative Living from Original Design*, connects humanity with Infinity to accomplish what Holy God has always intended, which is to encompass and unite Heaven and earth as one complete Circle of Life. These supernatural encounters I transcribe is by inspiration of Holy Spirit—2 Peter 1:20-21 2 Timothy 3:16-17. Therefore, in my wholehearted obedience to my Lord and my God to write this book, I am *a* **partaker of the Glory now being revealed**.

Through these God-selected Holy encounters God Almighty took me into, He is manifesting what already exists in the invisible realm into the visible realm of earth through the obedient actions of His Righteous ones to whom The Lord is openly revealing what to do and speak for Him. Therefore, what already exists as invisible in the Spirit realm is now operating in Holy ways and is becoming visibly operational on earth. In this, God Almighty is bringing into visibility and tangible form the fullness of His Manifest Creative Glory to make Himself known in wholeness and usefulness which fulfills His Originally Designed Intent to fill the whole earth with His Glory. When this occurs, evil is eliminated thus fulfilling God's Holy Intent.

It is not the purpose of this book to humanly explain the celestial encounters I experienced by the *Will* of Holy God. The purpose of this book is to show a Holy Creator Who intends for those He Created in His Image and Likeness to Creatively fulfill their Originally Designed Eternal Destiny. By humankind's obedience to use their innately-designed creative abilities, the heavens and the earth can be restored to Supreme God's Original Intent.

Because Holy God's Original Design and Plan for earth and the heavens has been perverted through evil intentions, Holy God is now in the process of restoring His Original Design for Heaven and earth to operate together in perfect harmony.

Creative God truly wants humankind, whom He Created in His Image and Likeness, to know how to permanently eliminate evil that stole their rulership of the heavens and earth which shut them down from creatively designing their environment for Good. Therefore, in accordance to His Perfectly preordained *Will*, Creative God of Heaven and earth is presently showing how He is displaying His Power that is eliminating evil in all its forms. Creative God is doing this by replacing evil ways through the creative ability He innately Designed in each human being.

Holy Divine occurrences are displayed throughout the entire Holy Bible and are recorded for our learning. God's Son, Jesus Christ, came from Infinity and became a human being by being born from the womb of a woman in order to display Holy Divine occurrences that are attainable for human beings. Jesus Christ, the Only Son of God, willingly said YES to His Father's request to become human flesh by the incarnation of a miraculous birth that causes Him to be both human being and Holy God all at the same time. **DO NOT** attempt to understand this with your mind. You can't.

Holy Divine encounters recorded in The Holy Bible were written especially for those who would be living at the time when evil was expressing its best shots. Creative God's specific time has arrived to fully reinstate and accomplish one Righteous Kingdom Rule between Heaven and earth. The evolution of evil has diminished Holy Knowledge almost to the point of annihilation.

Even so, in the midst of evil being permanently eliminated, Creative God is intervening and making Himself known in the fullness of Wisdom and Knowledge. Holy God's ordained time has arrived for Him to openly and visibly reveal how it is possible to Creatively exist both now and beyond the ages of time.

As you choose to train yourself in Godliness, the Holy accounts as documented in The Holy Bible along with what is written in this book, *Creative Living from Original Design*, come alive. There are as well other Holy books presently being written and published that The Lord is raising up to reveal Himself in the fullness of Revelation Knowledge and Wisdom.

I humbly, yet with Supreme God's Authoritative permission, record in this book, *Creative Living from Original Design*, some of the Holy encounters I personally experienced which reveal God's Holy Purpose of making Himself known in the Glory He has in Heaven and is presently transmitting onto earth at this time in history. These holy encounters align with Biblical Truth and Wisdom.

Supreme God's Holy Intent is for you to know with understanding that you were Originally Created with an innately-designed creativity that He fully intends for you to achieve so that you bring into existence what you create in the same way He does.

Supreme God envisioned the earth and the heavens and then spoke them into existence. All through The Holy Bible, Supreme God is inviting human beings Created like Himself to imitate Him in using their innately-Designed Creative ability in the same way He does which is to creatively create their desired intent by speaking what they envision into existence by the words they speak. His Righteous Purpose is for humankind to occupy Infinity free from sin and evil so Heaven and earth operate in one complete Circle of Life that brings Him Glory and humankind enjoyment.

Ponder these words in The Holy Bible taken from The Passion Translation:

*Lord, you know everything there is to know about me. You perceive every movement of my heart and soul, and you understand my every thought before it even enters my mind. You are so intimately aware of me, Lord.*

*You read my heart like an open book and you know all the words I'm about to speak before I even start a sentence!*

*You know every step I will take before my journey even begins. You've gone into my future to prepare the way, and in kindness you follow behind me to spare me from the harm of my past.*

*With your hand of love upon my life, you impart a blessing to me. Wherever I go, your hand will guide me, your strength will empower me. It's impossible to disappear from you or to ask the darkness to hide me.*

*You formed my innermost being, shaping my delicate inside and my intricate outside, and wove them all together in my mother's womb.*

*I thank you, God, for making me so mysteriously complex! How thoroughly you know me, Lord! You even formed every bone in my body when you created me in the secrete place, carefully, skillfully shaping me.*

*You saw who you created me to before I became me! Before I'd ever seen the light of day, the number of days you planned for me were already recorded in your book.*

*Every single moment you are thinking of me! How precious and wonderful to consider that you cherish me constantly in your every thought!*

*When I awake each morning, you're still with me.* (Psalm 139)

May each person reading this book be personally stimulated and invigorated to pursue Holy and Creative God to learn how they can creatively create their own unique personal environment and then join their personal creativity with the Holy creative ability of others and in agreed conjunction enjoy an enlightened Infinity.

The Lord God of Creation has openly revealed Himself to me since early childhood. I simply accepted Him each time He presented Himself to me. I openly and honestly convey Him in my writings as the only way I know to identify Him: Love and Truth.

The Lord Sovereignly trained me to know His Voice and His Holy Ways through His unchangeable Word by means of the Inspirational Power and Wisdom of Holy Spirit. Read

2 Timothy 3:16-17, 2 Peter 1:16-21, and Romans 15:4 in The Holy Bible. My personal Holy creative encounters align with His Holy Word of Truth as found in The Holy Bible. Holy God desires for each person to know Him in intimacy so they too can have their own personal celestial encounters with Him.

In all these Holy encounters, I personally interact with my Sovereign God whom I have known on intimate terms since early childhood when He came to me in an orphanage. In obedience to Him, I accurately record in this book some of my most recent Holy interactions with Him.

Holy God is revealing Himself to me according to His innately-Designed destiny for my life both now and for Infinity. What I write in this book are transcendent Holy celestial encounters He has allowed me to have a part in for His Purpose of revealing how Heaven and earth are to be reconciled so they operate as one complete Circle of Life throughout Infinity. I continuously agree to allow Him to Live and Move and have His Being in me and through me however He desires. I pray you, the reader, also allow The God of Infinity to work in you those things that are pleasing in His Sight so you can fulfill your intended and designed destiny.

My desire in all my writings is to accurately relate Holy God Who is Love and Truth as He has Sovereignly chosen to show Himself to me. He deeply desires to personally make Himself known to each and every person so that each of you fulfills your Creatively-Designed Destiny. I trust God of Love and Truth to reveal Himself to you in these writings in a way that is meaningful to you so that you Eternally fulfill the Holy destiny for which He Created you. May Creative God be truly Glorified as each one of us attains our Eternal Creative Destiny.

The Lord made it clear to me that what I am writing in this book is to be accomplished in cooperation together with those living in Highest Heaven with Him and those who live upon the earth. Keep in mind that to God, there is no separation (disconnection, detachment, severance, dissociation) between Heaven (Spiritual) and earth (natural).

What is vividly being made known in this book is to be distributed so that others know that Creative God is fulfilling the Truth He has spoken and revealed throughout all the ages of time. He is tangibly making Himself known on earth and in the heavens in powerful and noticeable ways. All that He has spoken and revealed through all the ages of time is being fulfilled because His Truth is founded on Wisdom and Revelation Knowledge based on His personhood.

Because evil intent has upset Creative God's Original Plan for Heaven and earth to cooperatively function together for Good, The Lord is Creatively revealing how He intends to restore and reconcile Heaven and earth back to His Original Intent so, together in harmony, Heaven and earth operate as one Holy Creation for Eternity.

*For He has made known to us, in all wisdom and insight the mystery of His Will, according to His purpose which He set forth in Christ as a plan for the fullness of time, to unite all things in Him, things in Heaven and things on earth.* (Ephesians 1:9–10 The Passion Translation)

*For in Him* [Christ Jesus] *all the fullness of God was pleased to dwell, and through Him to reconcile to Himself all things, whether on earth, or in Heaven, making peace by the Blood of His cross.* (Colossians 1:19–20)

Creative God's Holy Purpose for using Words and displaying tangible Actions is to cause redeemed people to learn how to regulate and maintain His Creatively-Designed Creation with Love, Authority, Justice, and Harmony that makes for an enjoyable Infinity.

I was pondering within myself how these personal celestial Holy encounters, which involve harmonious operations between Heaven and earth, would be understood as The Lord intends.

Eternal and Living God let me know that is not up to me whether or not His Creative Ways are understood. It's up to me to obey Him to publish these experiences so that His Creative Ways are known as to how Heaven and earth are to Creatively function for Infinity. He further made me to know that these supernatural or beyond natural activities He took me into are cooperative maneuvers that are to operate between Heaven and earth as one Holy and complete operation for Infinity. I willingly and continually submit to Him. I allow Him to continually reveal to me what I do not know that I need to know in order to bring Heaven and earth back into complete harmony to function as one complete Circle of Life for Eternity.

What I am writing in this book by the inspiration and direction of Holy God is to favorably and distinctly build an indisputable Foundation of Truth for others to build on who come after me.

Creative God is making Himself known through what I am writing in ways that He wants to be known. He is displaying His sure Foundation of Truth and Justice that opens Eternal Ways for Creative Living for those who fully desire to know Truth so they can creatively design and maintain their innately-desired intent that continues for

Infinity. Faithful obedience reaps rewards for those who obey what Creative God is revealing through these writings that honestly reveal His Holy way to achieve true and joyful living that lasts forever.

For these Truths to operate in one's life, it is imperative that each person makes a heart decision to receive Salvation from sin and evil that the Father offers through Jesus' Blood Sacrifice and as well wholeheartedly forgive all who have trespassed against you as Your Father in Heaven has totally forgiven you so you can receive from Him all you ask and desire. When this heartfelt and decisive choice is honestly made before Almighty God and publicly confessed before another person, then you have the ability to mature in Eternal Ways that can never be erased.

When you truly and honestly make this Eternal decision and so desire above all else that you want Holy God to be the Source of your Life, then His DNA (**divine nature assimilated**) lives in you and imparts His Wisdom Truth into you that continually empowers your RNA (**revealed nature achieved**) to creatively design and bring into existence your intended and good desires that fulfills your designed destiny.

Wisdom Truth is imprinted into your DNA (**divine nature assimilated**). Your **revealed nature achieved** is Holy God's innate DNA causing you to accomplish your designed destiny for the GOOD of His Creation and all humankind who He Created to be like Him in nature and ability.

This is an ongoing operation from intimate relationship with Him so you learn for yourself what your own personal design entails. The Father's DNA abiding in you causes you to be like Him in nature and ability which ignites your RNA to create from the original design He innately placed in you before you were ever born. What you design and create blesses your Father in Heaven and helps humankind.[1]

Holy God is a Father who delights in listening to His children He Created to be like Himself. He is a Good and Favorable Holy Being properly caring for His children He made to be like Himself. He endows them with Holy rule, dominion, and stewardship over whatever they creatively create to inhabit for Infinity.

Supreme and Living God knows you in the way He Created you to exist for Infinity, so He graciously and intimately interacts with you in your own personal way of communicating with Him. You just have to choose to do so. Don't allow yourself to be swayed from reaching out to Him no matter how weak your first attempts may be to know Him in ways you have not known Him. Ask Him honestly and openly to reveal Himself to you in Creative Ways. Keep on asking Him no matter how much you may *think* you know Him and His Ways. Asking Him for more Knowledge and Wisdom to use in Creative Ways is an ongoing Way of Life for Infinity. Start practicing!

Read on to find out how The Lord God of Creation wants to be known to those who choose to listen to Him with the purpose of obeying His Word of Truth and Wisdom.

Hear Him!
See Him!
Choose to obey Him!

---

[1] I highly recommend Lance Wallnau's teachings that train you how to connect the natural and supernatural realms into everyday existence to achieve what God has innately designed in you to accomplish both now and for Infinity in cooperation wIth Heaven and earth. www.lancewalnau.com.

# The Immeasurable Holy Operations of Supreme God

## Disruption of the Earth

Have you noticed! The world has gone crazy and is totally out of the control of any sort of significant law and order. Everyone living by the world's standards is doing whatever they think is right for them with no consideration of how others choose to live. Anarchy and chaos are overtaking and consuming any kind of decency and peaceful living that has been the norm for centuries. There is a heinous disregard toward any kind of legal authority and rule of order.

Is anyone asking, "Why is there all this disruption on earth? Is there any answer to counteract all this disruption?"

I want to offer the only meaningful and concrete answer that there is. In the beginning of what is commonly known as the world, a Supreme Creator defined immutable laws that were to be adhered to so that there would be no chaos and disorder on the earth and in the heavens He created to be lived in and to be ruled by Peace and Harmony. These immutable laws included set boundaries that formed a solid sense of rule and order.

I was asking The Lord why I was seeing storms, fires and winds, volcanoes, earthquakes, and rocks on and within the earth, as one violent operation, all seeming to erupt in violent upheaval all at the same time.

As I quietly waited in His Presence, I knew innately and emphatically that the earth is thrashing and convulsing as in the pains of birth. Through all this upheaval, Holy God is birthing His Kingdom Rule of Righteousness in the heavens and on the earth. He is causing all forms of evil entities to be vomited out of their secret hiding places where they think they cannot be seen and so cannot be detected.

The Lord flooded me with His Love assuring me that I do not need to fear all this disruption because these things have to happen so that Righteousness can reign on earth to displace all evil ways that keep people from fulfilling their designed destines He placed in them for the good of His Creations.

I began to praise Him for His Great Strength and Power. He made me to know deep within me that when Holy praises are given to Him, He is empowered even more to display His Authority in the face of His enemies and *all* their clandestine evil. I had an enlightened understanding that Holy Praise empowers Creative God to Act Judiciously. Holy Praise propels Him into Action. His Mighty Power Acts that are presently being seen on the earth flow out of the increased Holy praise being voiced on earth through the people who know Him on intimate terms. Along with Holy increased praise through His Holy people, Creation is crying out to their Creator. The maneuvers and operations of the winds and waves, thunder and lightning, and fire are giving Him praise. This is why the rocks are crying out and joining the praises of God's Holy people. God's Holy people's praises are combining with the praises and cries of His Holy Creation which empowers Him into full forward motion to rout out all evil entities from their hiding places.

I recognized The Lord was placing Truth inside me. He revealed to me that the earth is convulsing to rid itself of evil. Blood is crying out from the earth for vengeance. Lifeblood is a form of praise God hears that forces Him to Act in Holy Vengeance and Wrath against those who cause Lifeblood to be spilled.

Holy God, The Father, asked His only begotten Son to come on earth in human flesh and allow His Holy LifeBlood to be poured on the earth to pay the penalty for the sin of iniquity that invaded His creatively-Designed Creations. Yeshua or Jesus Christ, God's only Son, said a hearty YES and agreed with His Father to become the Holy Blood Sacrifice that would pay the penalty for the sin of iniquity that invaded His Creation. Because Jesus willingly agreed, The Father told His Son, *"Vengeance is Mine. I will repay, says The Lord."* The Father's time has come to express His Holy Vengeance against all wickedness and evil that caused His Holy Son's Precious LifeBlood to be spilt. Holy Justice demands retribution. The Father's Authorized Holy Vengeance is against all evil entities who caused His Son, whom He loves, to spill His Blood to redeem His Creation.

My Lord and my God, how excellent is Your Name and Your Word! We rejoice with You and exalt You before all the heavens and the earth. You alone are worthy of ALL Praise, Honor, and Glory. Be magnified in our praise and worship to You alone! Your Love to us empowers us to praise You even more. We join with Jesus in praising and thanking You for avenging His Holy Blood and for delivering us from all evil and for seating us with you in heavenly places to Rule and Reign with You in all Righteousness, Peace, and Joy. This is The Kingdom of God!

**God Is Working in Unseen Ways**

Holy God is working in Ways that cannot be seen by those who choose not to submit to His Way of doing things.

When you ask God to show you what He is doing on earth at this time, He will show you in unexpected ways. It won't necessarily be through pleasant ways. You must know that when your circumstances become unpleasant, God is carrying you and is with you to deliver you from what is coming against you. This is the time to intimately know God of Love and Truth so you can trust Him unreservedly. God is presently disrupting things the way we know them to be so He can get us to recognize the way we have been doing things is not working.

We must know that Holy angels are on assignment because people are crying out to God in their pain asking Him to help them. God is answering these prayers and bringing to us what is needed to accomplish His Creatively-Designed *Will*.

In the midst of unpleasant situations, learn to look for God's abundant Blessings He is pouring out on you to be far more than you expect or can contain. God intends for you to share these Blessings with others. However, you must keep your focus on God, not on the Blessing of provision just for the sake of having the Blessing. When you do this, the abundance of His Blessing of provision continue flowing and coming to you for His Purposes. You must know this and trust God. You should count on this as you trust God in what He is saying to do so that His *Will* is accomplished by what you say and do in obedience to His Holy directives.

### Partaking in God's Glory Being Revealed

God Almighty is manifesting what already exists in the invisible realm into the visible realm of earth through the obedient actions of His Righteous ones to whom The

Lord is openly revealing what to do and speak for Him. Therefore, what already exists as invisible in the Spirit realm is now operating in Holy ways and is becoming visibly operational on earth. In this, God Almighty is bringing into visibility and tangible form the fullness of His Manifest *Creative Glory* to make Himself known in wholeness and usefulness so the whole earth is filled with His Originally Designed Intent which shuts down all evil. Those who wholeheartedly obey The Lord are partaking in His Glory that is being revealed.

**Halting Old Methods**

The Lord opened up my understanding to know that upcoming generations are to be trained in His Creative Ways so that they follow their creative bent that He innately designed within them. He related to me that those who choose to operate in Creative Ways are stopping OLD methods and bringing in the NEW ways that are presently being released on earth. OLD ways and methods no longer work. NEW methods and ways must come forth to replace what people presumed would work but now recognize does not produce good and lasting results.

For NEW ways to be established, it is imperative not to look back or return to past ways. We must learn God's NEW ways and act in NEW ways that produce Good and lasting results.

What was done in the past is gone and so can never be repeated. When the NEW is being done congruently, it is being accomplished and lasts for Infinity. Creative God lives in Infinity where there is no past, present, or future.

Jesus said in The Holy Bible:
*Why do you keep looking backward to your past and have second thoughts about following me? When you turn back you are useless to God's kingdom realm* (Luke 9:62).

Lord, I choose to walk in Your Creative Glory expansion believing You to work in me and through me what I cannot accomplish without Your intervention. I rely on Your Glory Fire Presence working within me to flow out through me. I choose not to look at my circumstances on earth but to expect Your Holy Provision from Heaven to operate through me.

**Bringing in New Ways**

In order to walk into the NEW, our lives must be simplified. We must let go of OLD habits and ways of doing things. We cannot stay in OLD ways or the ways we are used to doing things, which includes daily chores. We must make a concrete effort to put into practice doing things that will bring His NEW ways into tangible manifestation.

Here are some practical checkpoints:

Pray daily and often!
Praise God continuously!
Trust God in all your ways!
Envision God's Divine Orders to you which determines your daily activities!
Cease from daily labors beyond what is necessary—let things go!
Do not allow yourself to deter from these practical checkpoints!
Do not speak unnecessary or idle words!

Speak Words of Authority that cause people and angels to help you!
Act in Love toward all people!

Daily refurbish these directives by integrating these practical ways into your everyday life so in the midst of your unsettling circumstances you align your life with God's Ways to truthfully live. Making a concerted effort to diligently practice these activities in your life causes you to go forward on a level path in accomplishing your divine destiny that is innately within you.

It is imperative that you allow God's thoughts and plans to be integrated into your life so you can fulfill your creatively-Designed Destiny that continues for Infinity. Make a quality decision within yourself to keep expanding yourself in God's Creative Design that is implanted in you by His doing.

Keep silent of all unnecessary or idle words so that when you do speak, the desires you want to occur flow and manifest into tangible form from your Holy intent. Keeping silent and not speaking unnecessary words continually increases Holy God's Creative Energy and Power so that when you do choose to speak into your circumstances, Holy Fire Power emanates from the sound waves in your voice that designs your Holy intent for the present and for Infinity.

These Holy operations cause you to recognize in fullness of understanding that when you speak and talk by God's Creative Glory residing in you, what you speak causes God's perpetual Creative Energy and Power to activate, which brings His Righteous Kingdom on earth. Then His Intended and Designed *Will* for redeemed humankind to rule the heavens and the earth in Holy Dominion both now and for Eternity can be accomplished.

God's time of acceleration for the expansion of His Creative Glory to operate on earth is here. Therefore, what has been known dimly can now be known in fullness so His Kingdom is established on earth to function as it functions in Highest Heaven. This expansion of God's Creative Glory fills the whole earth with His Knowledge and Glory and fills the whole earth with people who know Him.

## Written in God's Books

God has Books in Heaven that contain the record of His Originally Designed Ways He intends to be fulfilled. What is recorded in these Books in Heaven does not change. Therefore, God is seeing to it that all His Original Plans recorded in these Books is being made known at this time on earth so that what is written in the Books is accomplished and completed Forever.

What is written in some of these Books reveals your ordained destiny that Holy angels can go to and see what is written about you so they can then arrange your circumstances for these to be fulfilled. You may ask God to send His Holy angels assigned to you to go and open your Book to see what is written about you that needs to be done so you can fulfill your Creatively Designed Destiny.

Each person's destiny is written in the books, and there is more than one book written about each person. You have a book with your name on it that contains and reveals your ordained destiny that Holy angels can go to and see what God has written in your book for you to accomplish.

Your circumstances are arranged by God and His Holy angels to assist you in fulfilling your ordained destiny.

However, there are other books written pertaining to your responses to God's directions to you. These other books record your obedient actions and your rewards for faithfulness and obedience to Holy God.

There are also other books carrying God's Designed *Will* that reveal your assignments He has ordained for you to do in accomplishing His Designed *Will*. There are created beings Designed by Supreme God who carry Wisdom and Prudence. You can call on Wisdom and Prudence to enlighten what you don't know that you need to know. Then these books can be opened to reveal what is written in them for you to do. This is to be done when activities on earth dictate that it is time to fulfill what God has written in His Designed-*Will* Book that you need to carry out for His Glory to be known and seen on earth that dispels evil.

Lord, I ask You to put in my heart the desire to ask You what is written in the Books for me to accomplish for Your Glory and Honor. You are surely worthy of Praise. How Awesome and Magnificent You are, Lord! There is none like You. Show me what is written in the Books, Lord. Thank you.

## Manifest Glory Operations

Holy God is no longer acting in former ways. OLD ways have ceased through God's divinely appointed interference. God is once again unleashing on earth His Creative and Original Ways. He is presently bringing His Original

Ways of operating on earth back into public view. There are those who recognize that their way of thinking and doing no longer works. Therefore, they are ready to change their former habits and thinking to align with God's Original Way for them to creatively function on earth and in Heaven.

Holy God's Original and Creative Ways can operate through each person who allows themselves to trust Him and also trust themselves in working out how to incorporate and release their Creatively Designed Holy destiny. Through each redeemed person using their innate God-given creative ability, the earth and the heavens are being restored, renewed, and replenished to function as Supreme God Originally Designed.

O, Lord my God, I trust You, and I choose to trust myself as I pursue using the Creative Design you placed in me before I was born. Keep me from all forms of pride and deception so I can serve You in uprightness and prosperity all my days to make You known in all Your Glory and Power. Thank You.

**Molecular Restructure**

Beginning in January 2018, God's Holy Presence came into my home and remained for three months. His Presence was so heavy and powerfully within in me, upon me, and around me in my home that I could barely function in the natural.

During this three-month timeframe in 2018, God's Holy Presence was tangibly and powerfully evident in my home. One morning I awoke overpowered by God's tangible Presence. I was stunned to the point of numbness and inability to do daily tasks of getting ready for a new day. I pushed on through to do the things that had to be done and then went to my Prayer Room. I said, "Why is this happening to my body? Why am I so physically stunned like this, Lord?"

The Lord caused me to know that He was restructuring the molecular structure system of my body so He could take me where He wants me to go to accomplish a higher purpose He has for taking me into places. I asked Him why He was doing this to me.

He let me know that He was doing this so my body can transport back and forth from earth to Heaven in a transformed molecular structure to accomplish a purpose He had for me to do what I could not otherwise do without a molecular structure in my body. I asked if this meant I was going to die. He assured me that I would not die the way I was thinking. I knew by Holy Spirit that my body, soul, and spirit would still be intact so I could properly function both in Heaven and on earth.

Therefore, I submitted to Holy God. I knew Him so well in full trust and assurance that I knew this was from Him for me to do. Therefore, I gave God permission to work in me whatever pleases Him in using me as He *Wills*. I chose not to stop this flow of Power and Authority that was transforming the molecular structure of my body. I expressed to The Lord that I would receive all He was doing in me, around me, and through me for His Holy Purposes.

I fully trusted Holy God in releasing myself to Him and in allowing Him to transform my molecular structure to operate in higher degrees of Creative Glory. I cannot explain this nor do I totally understand this. I just yielded in worship to my God who I fully trusted. I was immensely enjoying His Holy Glory Fire Presence that was in me and all around me. He supplied the Strength I needed to do ordinary tasks when I needed to. To Supreme God alone be all the Honor and Glory forever and ever! This encounter and others of like nature that The Lord has taken me into since childhood, are detailed in this author's book, *Infinite Destiny: Truth and Wisdom*.

I know in Truth and with understanding that The Lord restructured my physical body in a higher molecular form to carry in fullness the Power and Authority of Heaven so that when He transports me by Holy Spirit encounters to be on the scene in the Spiritual realm or in natural situations where He wants to bring change for Good that what I obey Him to do in cooperation with Him is accomplished. The Holy Bible gives accounts of this happening with Elijah and Philip, Jesus, and Paul for whatever Good purpose our Father in Heaven had for their encounters.

**Greater Works**

I asked The Lord how I was to do the works that Jesus did: disappear into the clouds and vanish, walk out of the midst of a crowd when people were trying to kill him, come back and forth from Heaven to earth as He has openly revealed to me are the...*greater works*... Jesus said we would be doing to bring Supernatural Acts on earth to make Almighty God known in all His Glory and Power to shut down Satan's evil.

I have read about Kathryn Kuhlman's life that when she walked into a place, people would be powerfully influenced and touched by Holy Spirit sometimes without her saying a word. I have never understood how this could happen. I always pondered how this happens and to some degree asked for this to occur for me even though I had no understanding how this could happen. I recognize now that The Lord was revealing a foretaste that this is indeed possible. The circumstances on earth are such that He is manifesting the fullness of supernatural happenings through obedient people so wickedness and evil is kept from being dominant, and His Glory is manifested in Influential Power.

There are Holy Bible accounts of Jesus when He lived on earth at times vanishing out of the midst of a crowd of people who were trying to kill him and after He was resurrected from death disappearing into the clouds ascending back into Heaven. Paul, the apostle, had an encounter in the third heaven and came back to earth and gave an account of what happened to him in the best way he could explain. He just honestly told what he knew happened to him even though he did not fully understand.

Jesus spoke that we who would come after Him would do... *greater works*...than He did because He was going back to His Father in Heaven and would send Holy Spirit who would live in us permanently, and therefore, we would do even greater works than He did. Jesus knew His Father's *Will* and knew the time would come when these supernatural occurrences would need to be done to save many people's lives during the time Satan was attempting to annihilate and destroy people and everything on earth so he could rule a kingdom of his own making.

When evil operations are taking place on earth, trusting God to work through miraculous ways is a must so that He can be seen and known in Power manifestations that outdo Satan. Even though Satan is permitted to do supernatural things, God Almighty is greater than anything Satan could ever do.

The times we are currently living through dictate that Holy God is doing supernatural occurrences that are greater than Satan's evil to show Himself as Supreme God over all forms of wickedness and evil.

How marvelous are Your Ways in our eyes, O Lord.

## Gabriel Brings Visionary Glory Box

During this time of intense Holy Presence in my home in 2018, I awoke at 2:15 a.m. worshipping The Lord expressing my love to Him. As I lay in bed, I saw a Pure White substance. I could not distinguish exactly what it was.

I became aware of an angel I saw way up high in the heavens. He was Pure White and had wings. He was wearing a Pure White robe with his knees bent like he was carrying something. He emerged out of a Pure White Substance that appeared to me to be a Glory Cloud. Then I saw another Pure White object shaped in rectangle form also emerging out of this Pure White Substance pointing downward as if coming down toward earth from Heaven. I knew this angel was coming to me and bringing me this rectangle Box. I was puzzled by what I saw.

I asked The Lord to reveal to me what I was seeing. He related to me that this was an angel coming to me emerging from Pure White Substance and bringing me a Box containing Visionary Glory. The Lord said I could open this Box anytime I wanted.

I asked, "What is Visionary Glory?"

The Lord openly revealed to me that Visionary Glory is Living Substance. Visionary Glory exists in the Spirit realm and is actual Living Substance. The Substance of Life exists in reality form in the invisible Spirit realm and can be brought into tangible manifestation by calling into being with words what is seen from Visionary Glory so that what could not be seen before can now be seen and known. Visionary Glory is actual Living Substance that can be displayed into material manifestation by spoken words. I suddenly understood that the words I regularly declare *I release the Glory Influence to displace the powers of darkness and replace them with the Ruling Presence of Almighty and Living God* are actually manifesting Living Visionary Glory Substance on earth to displace evil operations.

Visionary Glory is Living Substance that can be seen and acted upon. It is real, not imagined. When the Box containing Visionary Glory is opened, what is seen from Visionary Glory can be brought into our circumstances and as well over situations we hear about in the natural. We are to do or act on what is seen from Visionary Glory which is Living Substance.

By acting on what is seen from Visionary Glory, Living Substance is brought on earth from Heaven that displays God's Justice on earth. We are to call those things that are not seen in the natural as though they are because these things that are invisible to us on earth exist as Living Substance. These invisible things exist as Living Substance and can come into visible form to be used on earth for Good purposes. This is accomplished by words that are spoken from what is seen from Visionary Glory. It is God's Holy *Will* that this be done in order to displace the powers of darkness. It must be made known that what is seen from Visionary Glory is actual Living Substance that is to be spoken into existence on earth to exalt Holy God and eradicate Satan's evil.

Visionary Glory is increased as we obey and go and do what Holy God is revealing must be done in our circumstances. Visionary Glory guides us in seeing what to do or say in every situation or circumstance we are in or up against. We are to count on this and act like Visionary Glory is there because it is. If we don't act like Visionary Glory is there, it remains invisible and unusable and therefore cannot be used as God intends for it to be used for His Holy Purpose of eradicating evil in all its forms.

Visionary Glory is invisible Living Substance that is alive and active and can materialize into tangible matter to be used on earth in our circumstances when what is seen from Visionary Glory is spoken into actual existence. What is seen from invisible Visionary Glory can be spoken into visible form that is fully operational on earth. Elijah, Elisha, and Jesus operated from Visionary Glory to do what seemed to be miracles to people on earth but is who God is—the Great I AM to whom nothing is impossible. Visible and invisible are both alike to Him.

Holy God is in the process of merging both visible and invisible realms back to the Original State of Glory before Satan disrupted His Designed Plan for earth. There was no visible and invisible in Creation until Satan flaunted his rebellion before humankind, and they accepted this rebellion as reality. Rebellion forced Holy God to conceal invisible Glory Substance from visible form so that what intrinsically resides in Glory Substance could not be used for evil purposes. Humankind became content to accept only operating in visible form when there is so much more available to them to be used for good purposes and holy reasons that enables visible and invisible realms to manifest as one complete and holy operation. Nevertheless, Supreme God already had a set Plan in motion to reconcile and reestablish visible and invisible realms as one complete operation so that evil would not remain forever and so stop God's Holy Creative Designed Plan for people's lives that goes on for Infinity.

Holy God's predetermined time has come to reconcile and restore the visible and invisible realms to function from Original Design in operating as one solitary complete operation. God's Holy Purpose for Heaven and earth to function together as one fluid operation Originated from His Uniquely Designed Purpose He formed before the foundation of the world. Jesus' Holy Blood Sacrifice redeemed humankind to live in Visionary Glory. Those who accept God's Holy Redemption from evil and walk with Him in Blood Covenant relationship have the ability to operate from Visionary Glory *if* they so choose. In order for Visionary Glory to operate in the Way God Purposed from the beginning of time, redeemed people must choose to operate in Visionary Glory. At this time on earth, Visionary Glory operations must be activated so that every form of dark and perverse evil is permanently eradicated.

Ask Holy God to grant you fullness of understanding from Revelation Knowledge and Wisdom to know how to creatively operate in Visionary Glory. When you act in accordance to what He reveals to you, you receive what you ask of Him.

As I was compiling and recording all The Lord is speaking to me, *suddenly*, understanding opened to me. Instantly, I knew that the angel descending to me with a Pure White

Box containing Visionary Glory Substance was Gabriel. In this Visionary Glory Box Gabriel brought to me are the Good things or works that God Planned before the foundation of the world that are to be accomplished at this time on earth when God's Word of Authority is being fulfilled by His doing.

Visionary Glory is Living Substance which can be Creative words or acts in the form of words, pictures, prayer to verbalize, specific healing pronouncements, a Blessing, a Righteous Judgement announcement. When the Glory Box containing Visionary Glory Substance is opened, what is seen from Visionary Glory can be released into your immediate circumstances, or over situations you hear about, or in which you are personally involved by God's doing. By speaking or acting on what you see in the Visionary Glory Box, Holy Creative acts are being performed by the words you speak and the actions you perform.

Remember when you were a child and imagined all kinds of things—that your teddy bear or superman doll could hear you and knew what you were saying or that you could fly or jump off a tall building and land on your feet in one piece without any kind of harm or walk on or lay down on white clouds in the sky. When I fly in airplanes, I still imagine myself playing on the white puffy clouds. Well, transfer this into using your imagination to design, frame, and speak into reality existence what you imagine. God Created this innate ability in us to imagine and create into existence what we envision. This is why young children are so tuned into their imagination. They so want what they imagine to be real just as you did when you were a child. If you have young children, encourage them to develop their imagination to dream and to integrally form into actual manifestation what they see inside them that to them is real because it is real. Visionary Glory that Holy God innately Created within each human being is to be used for good purposes, and not for evil purposes.

God, The Great I Am, has no limits as to how to release and transport Visionary Glory, which is Living Substance. As you ask Him to know, when you are in a situation you need to know, you will know what word or act needs to operate in the situation you find yourself. Then you step out and do what you know to do trusting Visionary Glory to operate and meet the need at hand.

God's Visionary Glory Substance is amazing and overwhelms our finite minds. We must trust and rely on God's Holy Wisdom to empower us to obey what we see and know to do from Visionary Glory, which is Living Substance that sustains Life.

O, Lord, comprehension of Your Visionary Glory Substance is amazing and is overwhelming to our finite minds. We trust and rely on Your Holy Wisdom to empower us to obey You. Thank You for revealing Yourself to us in Visionary Glory, which is Living Substance that sustains Life. I thank and praise You, God of my life.

**Invisible Substance of Life—Material Manifestation**

Substance of Life resides in Holy Spirit who essentially exists in The Father and in Jesus, His Only Son. If we love God and keep His commandments, Father, Son, and Holy Spirit abides in us, and we abide in Him (Galatians 2:20). Jesus said to His disciples,

*Loving Me empowers you to obey My word. And My Father will love you so deeply that we will come to you*

*and make you our dwelling place. When the Father sends the Spirit of Holiness, the one like Me who sets you free, He will teach you all things in My name.* (John 14:23-26, 17:20-23)

Therefore, we who are created in Holy God's Image and Likeness can create material matter from the Substance of Life that exists in the invisible realm by Jesus' Faith, abiding in us. Jesus' Faith abiding in us enables us to believe in Holy Spirit's Creative Ability to operate The Father's *Willed* Design through us.

Jesus manifested The Father's Substance of Life innately residing in Him when He spoke into visible form what appeared to be invisible: water into wine, expansion of food. Jesus' spoken words caused the water to become wine and food to multiply so that the Substance of Life would manifest into useable material form on earth. Jesus' spoken words caused water to become solid matter for Him to walk on, bread and fish to multiply, and people to come back to Life from the dead. Jesus did many other things that are not recorded in the Bible according to John 21:25.

Jesus Created what was needed in a situation by *Faith* in His Father's and Holy Spirit's Ability to manifest tangible matter from The Substance of Life residing in them. Jesus knew His Father and Holy Spirit dwelled in Him also. Jesus knew that when He spoke from the Substance of Life residing in His Father and Holy Spirit and in Him as well, the very thing He spoke that was tangibly alive in Heaven but was invisible on earth would manifest into tangible matter that would sustain Life on earth. Faith manifests invisible substance into visible matter. Faith acts upon what is genuinely believed.

From this Truth, those redeemed by Jesus' Blood Sacrifice who freely choose to speak and act by Jesus' Faith abiding in them can create material matter from the invisible Substance of Life. When we truly believe Jesus' Faith abides in us, then we can step out in Jesus' Faith and creatively speak into material existence the tangible objects we desire to exist in our environment that brings us enjoyment.

I know by Holy revelation knowledge that we who are Created in True God's Likeness and Image can create things from Visionary Glory which intrinsically is Substance of Life Who resides in The Father as Holy Spirit and Jesus and flows out from them into those who are redeemed by Jesus' Precious Blood so together as one Holy operation Creative manifestations come into existence to be joyfully used for God's Glory and Pleasure as well as for our benefit and enjoyment.

The Substance of Life is invisible until we speak into tangible existence whatever words or material objects we see from Visionary Glory and then speak into material existence. What exists in the invisible realm and we see by Visionary Glory comes into existence on earth by our Holy creative desires and spoken words. We must truly *believe* that we can create what we desire by Jesus' Faith permanently residing in us who are redeemed by Jesus' precious Blood sacrifice. Therefore, we can accept with *no doubting* that it is Jesus' Faith in us doing the creative work through us (Galatians 2:20). When we truly believe and act from this premise, Supreme God's inherent creativity indwelling us cannot be affected by Satan's evil influence. We are Holy as He is Holy with the ability to Create our environment as we desire. Supreme God Created the heavens and the earth for humankind to rule and have dominion over by the words He spoke. Consider what is written in The Holy Bible in Isaiah 65:17-25, Psalm 8, Hebrews 2:1-9, 1 Peter 1:13-21.

*Faith* is tangible reality that exists in the actual Substance of Life and is what causes material things we desire that are yet in vision form to manifest into material manifestation that can be used on earth. The capacity to create comes from your innate Holy passionate desire that flows from faith, which is actual Living Substance.

When you are born again into New Life in Christ Jesus (John 3:3-8), the law of the Spirit of the Life of Christ Jesus lives in you enabling you to creatively create what you envision that is innately within you for you to draw from (Psalm 139). Ruminate and digest Romans 4-8.

Your passionate desire is outlined in vision form from your innate creativity or imagination that Holy God Creatively Designed in you before you were born. Your creative vision emanates into material manifestation from the Holy words you speak and actions you perform by Jesus' faith residing in you, which is Living Substance. Your Holy innate desire sees what you want from your creative imagination and so forms into material manifestation by the words you speak. To be specific, Your Holy words emanate and materialize or manifest into visible form from the innate desire that is in your heart. This innate desire is formed by your creative imagination residing in the Substance of Life known as faith. What you form and create from Living Faith is to be used for Good.

Our innate desire to generate what we creatively envision by Holy Spirit's Substance of Life transports the invisible structure of what we envision into visible manifestation and testifies to the innate creativity Supreme God Designed in us before we were born (Psalm 139). What we speak from the Living Substance of Life from the faith of Father, Holy Spirit, and Jesus indwelling us is what opens up to us the realm of Visionary Glory Influence that brings into material existence on earth what we create with our words from the Substance of Life Who is the very Source of Originality.

Holy God's Creative Glory Influence is Favor. Favor is an actual Living Substance that truly exists in the invisible realm in visible form and must be called into manifestation from our desired intent and spoken words. God's Creative Glory Influence transposes the Substance of Life into material manifestation on earth by our desired intent and our spoken words. Favor is a Living Substance that causes the atoms that make up the physical world to respond to our spoken words.

Whatever we construct from our Holy creative imagination and then speak into existence from Visionary Glory issues from the Substance of Life and so structures or forms into visible manifestation the Holy creative words we speak that can be used on earth for good.

Our innate Holy desire to create what we envision creatively frames what is invisible to us but has not yet been Created into material matter. Creating into material manifestation what we creatively envision is possible through our confident expectation or hope that this is possible through the *Faith* of Jesus and His Father and Holy Spirit indwelling us. *Faith* is a Living Substance that permanently resides in The Father, Holy Spirit, and in His Son Who indwell us. Therefore, our *hope* or confident expectation is anchored on their *Faith* indwelling us. Thereby, we positively know our desired intent is certainly being fulfilled. We frame our Holy desired intent from what we see from Visionary Glory. Then we bring into material manifestation our desired intent from the Substance of Life residing in Father, Son, and Holy Spirit by the words we speak through the Faith of The Father, Jesus, and Holy Spirt indwelling us.

**Living Substance in invisible form is still tangible matter that can be spoken into material manifestation into the earth through the emanating Substance of Life abiding in Father, Holy Spirit, and Jesus Who indwells each true believer who trusts and relies on Holy God and His Holy Word.**

Engage yourself to come into The Father's Presence and profess that Jesus' Blood Sacrifice stands for you on the Mercy Seat allowing you direct access to your Heavenly Father. From intimate relationship by being in The Father's Very Presence, you participate with Him in creating into tangible manifestation what you see by Visionary Glory that exists in invisible form within The Substance of Life. This is what is better understood as procreating with The Father to generate Holy Life or Fruit into the earth and the heavens that remains Eternally.

What you see from Visionary Glory is the Substance of Life that essentially exists in The Father who dwells within you. From Visionary Glory emanating from the Substance of Life, you speak with words your intended desire you want to bring into material manifestation. What you frame from Visionary Glory actualizes into visible matter that can be used on earth by what you see in invisible form from being in The Presence of The Father's Voice. This is to be an ongoing operation causing material things to happen around your life for Eternity. This is how you procreate with Holy God throughout Infinity.

The Father's Voice has a unique pattern which is the Source of Creative Origin. Sound is the Pattern of The Father's Voice which forms a frequency that attracts to Original Design. Matter can only be created from The Substance of Life residing in The Father (Genesis 1). When you are in the Presence of The Father, you learn to know His Voice and so can creatively speak from within His Voice speaking to you. From the words that you hear or see from within His Voice, you speak. What you speak has the ability to creatively form tangible matter that emanates from The Substance of Life residing in Father, Holy Spirit, and Jesus. Your voice emanating or coming from within His Voice is what brings into material existence on earth what you frame by your Holy words because Father, Jesus, and Holy Spirit's residing Presence indwells you, and so you are in Him, and He is in you (John 17:21–23).

Because Jesus' *Faith* resides in us along with the indwelling Life of Father and Holy Spirit, we have the intrinsic and essential belonging ability from our Holy position in Jesus to be able to procreate with our Father in creating our Holy desired intent that formulates into visible manifestation by the Holy Words we speak.

Thank You, Lord, for showing me Truth about Visionary Glory. Now that I understand how Visionary Glory operates, I ask You for an increase of Visionary Glory to use on earth to displace the powers of darkness in every situation I find myself or I observe or You send me or take me.

## Invisible Atoms, DNA, and Transmuted RNA

In the invisible Spirit realm, tangible atoms formulate from Living Substance and produce Life in invisible form that are undetected to us who live in the physical realm on earth, but nevertheless, tangibly exist in the invisible realm. Invisible atoms are actual Living Substance that truly exist. From this undeniable Truth, invisible atoms are to be observed by the *Faith* of Father, Holy Spirit, and Jesus permanently residing in redeemed humankind. When these invisible atoms are observed, the actual Living Substance that is invisible to us on earth is to be brought into material manifestation by pure and holy words of decree and creatively designed actions so that the innately Creative destinies God innately designed in humankind can be performed on earth and for Infinity.

The Creative ability for humankind to Create as Supreme God Creates comes from DNA (*divine nature assimilated*) transmuted into RNA (*revealed nature achieved*). Therefore, because humankind is Created in Holy God's Image and after His Likeness, they too can create in the same Way He Creates. Supreme God Creates from what He speaks from The Substance of Life that essentially resides within Himself, and also resides in Holy Spirit and in Jesus, His Only Son who altogether abides in us.

Therefore, the innate DNA (*divine nature assimilated*) and RNA (*revealed nature achieved*) abiding in redeemed humankind must flow together in harmony to be able to bring invisible substance into tangible matter and form to be used on earth. This harmonious action engages Spirit world with physical world to bring the Kingdom of God that exists in invisible form in Heaven into the material realm on earth to become the visible Kingdom of God on earth*divine nature assimilatedrevealed nature achieved*.

*Faith* and *hope* are RNA (*revealed nature achieved*) and is the building block that sets every material thing in place and holds together the structure of our spoken Holy words. From RNA, the creatively created object can be visibly manifested on earth by the Holy words we speak from The Father, Holy Spirit, and Jesus' *faith* abiding in us Who has the essential ability to manifest into visible manifestation our heart's intent and desire. DNA (*divine nature assimilated*) in us manifests what we frame by our Holy words from RNA (*revealed nature achieved*) in us.

From this reality, you can have confidence that Supreme God's DNA (*divine nature assimilated*) lives in you by Jesus' *Faith* indwelling you that reveals to you that He and The Father and Holy Spirit reside within you, and so you are one with Him. Therefore, you can truly believe Jesus' *Faith* abiding in you is DNA (*divine nature assimilated*) that is transforming within you as RNA (*revealed nature achieved*).

Consequently, from this Holy position of relationship through Jesus' Living Faith abiding in you, DNA (*divine nature assimilated*) becomes RNA (*revealed nature achieved*) that is exhibited through you.

Therefore, you have the essential ability to creatively design whatever you imagine and structure by the holy words of decree you speak and the inventive actions you perform from what you see by Visionary Glory*divine nature assimilatedrevealed nature achieved*.

At Moses' request, "*Show me Your Glory*," Holy God revealed His Glory to Moses. Supreme God responded to Moses' request by saying, *I will make my Goodness go before You...* (Exodus 33:18–19). God's Glory is His Goodness. God of Glory wants to be known as I Am who I Am Who is Goodness Personified. Therefore, everything Holy God does and speaks lines up with His Goodness. Therefore, Holy God abiding in you and you abiding in Him manifests His Goodness residing in you that becomes affirmative action by the holy words of decree you speak and the creative actions you take.

## Drawing on God's Glory Substance

In a dream, I saw a tube shaped in bent form with each end open. I saw a creamy white substance in the tube. I saw people activity but cannot remember the details.

I asked The Lord why the tube was shaped like this? Why was it not straight?

Holy God revealed in my heart that He does not pour Glory Substance into people until they seek Him. Each person redeemed by Jesus' Holy Blood Sacrifice who personally seeks to know Living God by choosing to live in His Presence, can draw on His Glory Substance as one would draw substance from a drinking straw. Those who choose to live in His Presence can draw on His Glory Substance that empowers them to speak holy words of decree and to perform creative actions by Glory Fire Power that dispels darkness and compels Light to perform everlasting Life in them.

## Gabriel Brings Glory Fire Messages

I awoke feeling myself smiling widely. Then I saw a head and face pop and vanish before my visionary eye space. This head had dark brown curly hair and the face was translucent white. I thought, *It's Gabriel! The angel of God's Presence.*

Because of previous Holy encounters with the angel of God's Presence, Gabriel, I knew this was Gabriel bringing

Glory Fire Messages to me. Gabriel carries God's Holy Fire Presence and expounds His Messages of Authority that Holy God wants disseminated. These Messages of Authority ignite and release Glory Fire Power, causing people living in sin to hear and recognize Holy God's Message to them. *If* they choose to respond to God's Authority Message to them, they receive Holy Power that changes their circumstances by empowering them to walk out of darkness and come into His Marvelous Light of Truth and Love that has everlasting benefit. The freewill choices each person makes whether good or evil establishes their temporary and Eternal destiny.

Glory Fire operations are God's intentional doing, not any person's. As people truly desire and then allow God's Holy Fire to demolish all that has consumed their thoughts and emotions based on lies causing deep-seated pain, they are set free. These ingrained deceptive thoughts and false beliefs have set up an idol in their heart that has replaced True God in their lives. God's Holy Glory Fire consumes all the dross within people's lives when they truly want these things removed from their lives and so prove this by turning to Him asking for His help.

When God's Word is spoken, Glory Fire is triggered causing sparks to fly that ignites stony hearts triggering slumbering people to seek God above all else. When those hearing the words of Truth, Light, and Life you speak and then seek True God with all their heart, they will find Him. Holy words of Life spoken by decree and performed by creative action exposes the devil's darkness in people and encases these lies with Holy Glory Fire Power that consumes deceptive lusts embedded within them, stemming from deeply rooted wrong beliefs and unholy desires. When people who have been held captive by unholy desires and wrong beliefs are set free because of seeking Holy God with all their heart, Glory Fire Power continuously operates around them so former ways of darkness can never return to harass them if they continue to live in holiness and Truth.

God's Voice carries Holy Fire. Holy Glory Fire ignites and consumes all that is not of God. God's Love is a burning Fire that cannot be quenched. His Holy Fire consumes all it touches with either all-consuming passionate Love for Him or death, which is Eternal separation from Him. Gods' Glory Fire causes people to make a freewill choice to either choose Eternal Life or Eternal death. Each person freely chooses how they respond to God.

Holy Glory Fire is Passionate Love personified igniting people to choose to walk in God's Ways of Holy Living *if* they will. That is why God is seen as a Pillar of Fire, and people feel as if Fire is burning within them. This Glory Fire is a Holy Fire of consuming Passion that is Pure and all-consuming burning up all that is not of God.

God's Holy Glory Fire replaces the passionate fire of lust and self-gratification that holds people captive to deception and lies. God's Holy Glory Fire burns out this dross and replaces it with His Passionate Love that remains within them. Holy Fire is Love that produces tangible manifestations of Life and Truth.

Each person who is cleansed by God's Holy Fire is now free to offer God unending praise, worship, and thanksgiving for eternally delivering them from false beliefs and the idols embedded in their hearts that were taking them away from Living God Who Loves them with passionate and Everlasting Love.

Pure and Holy worship expressed to God allows Him to act in agreement with your personal praise and worship to Him, and this is what restores Heaven and earth as one complete circle of Life as He Originally Designed.

True unadulterated worship that focuses on True God allows you to eat from the... *Tree of Life*...from which all Created Substance flows. Eating from the... *Tree of Life*... truly Creates unending Life and productivity.

Eating from the... *Tree of Life*...enables you to create what you desire. Eat and create! Eat and create is the way of Life throughout Eternity. Worship sustains Life forever. The fig tree refused to worship God, and it withered and died permanently for not bearing fruit that remains. This fig tree failed to transmit a message God Commanded it to give.

Consider this, your Pure unadulterated worship to Holy God exposes evil entities who defy Supreme God that causes them excruciating and unending torture because they wrongly desire to be worshipped. Continual pure Praise and Worship to the Lord God of heaven and earth tortures them even more. So bring even more pure praise and worship to Holy God. This pleases Him and blesses you.

**The Council of the Godly**

There are those in Heaven who are seated in the Council of the Godly in the Court of Heaven at the request of Holy Spirit. Those from earth who are brought into this Council at the request of Holy Spirit join the Council of the Godly in Heaven. This is a joint operation between Heaven and earth. This Council cooperates together to fulfill God's Purpose of Ruling His Righteous Kingdom as one complete Circle of Life.

Those living on earth who are being led by The Spirit of Holy God hear His summons to join Heaven's Council of the Godly. From this Holy encounter, they make a free-will decision to come into this Council and join with Heaven's Council of the Godly. All those attending this Council are held accountable by Almighty God.

God says in His Holy Word,

*Bring all who claim Me as their God, for I have made them for My Glory. It was I who Created them. Bring out the people who have eyes but are blind, who have ears but are deaf. Gather the nations together! Assemble the peoples of the world! Understand that I alone am God. There is no other God. There never has been, and there never will be. I, yes, I am The Lord, and there is no other Savior. From eternity to eternity I am God. No one can undo what I have done.* (Isaiah 43:8–9a, 10–11, 13 NLT)

As it is in Heaven so it is on earth. The Court of Heaven has Judged Satan forgotten forever. Therefore, Satan can never again attack or accuse anyone on earth or in Heaven who legally stands in Jesus' Judicial Blood Sacrifice that covers their sins in the Court of Heaven forever.

It has been decided in the Court of Heaven that the devil and all his evil is to be abolished in the...*lake of fire*... Therefore, no longer do people have to continually deal with evil. They can permanently live in Peace, Joy, Love, Harmony, and Rest with Holy God and others of like mind and heart in conjunction with all God's Creations of Beauty. Those who belong to God and so have cast away their self-desires and unholy ways have willingly chosen to forsake self-promotion and unholy ways. Therefore, they are no longer subject to Satan's attacks and unwarranted accusations before Heaven's Judicial Court. Through the judicial acts of redeemed people in cooperation with the Court of Heaven, Satan is permanently banned from the Court of Heaven. These combined Holy Judicial acts ensure Satan's Eternal annihilation. The Court in Heaven operates throughout Eternity.

Holy God is divulging secret things at this time of events on earth so people know that Life is never-ending and that their lives have a purpose whether they are living on earth or in Heaven. Redeemed people made in God's Image and after His Likeness rule from Heaven's Courts whether they are abiding on earth or in Heaven. Heaven's Court operates eternally.

Revelation knowledge originates from the Substance of Life that is now being unveiled and revealed for end-time operations between Heaven and earth. Therefore, Revelation knowledge originating from the Substance of Life operates through those who have ears to hear and eyes to see what Holy Spirit is doing through them and this is what transmits a tangible witness of observable holy operations between Heaven and earth. Heaven and earth work in cooperation to establish God's Righteous Kingdom on earth and in the heavens.

What Holy God is presently revealing is true and stands in His Council of Justice and can never be changed. People on earth need to truly recognize this. When they do, Heaven and earth can operate as one complete operation with no apparent separation. When the devil and all his evil activity is shut down, Holy God is Glorified forever and ever! Praise and thank Him for this!

Your Ways are unsearchable, O God of Heaven and earth. I give all praise and thanksgiving, honor, and Glory to You alone, O Lord of Might and Power.

## What Do Angels Know

The Lord caused me to know that people and angels learn and grow together to enhance each other. People and angels working in cooperation exchange with each other to gain fuller knowledge and understanding as to how to collaborate in performing His *Will* on earth and in the heavens. These operations between people and God's Holy angels in Heaven are increasing in greater dimensions and are releasing unveiled Truth from Heaven.

These joint Heaven and earth operations are bringing back into alignment God's Circle of Life to complete His Original Intention for Heaven and earth to exist as one Holy and comprehensive operation. The combined obedience between Heaven's angels and redeemed people on earth immensely blesses God.

Lord, I willingly join and cooperate with Your Holy Created angels and beings in performing Your Holy *Will* on earth and in the heavens. Be Blessed, our Lord and our God, in our combined obedience to You.

## Procreating by Perverted Angels

While in my kitchen preparing my breakfast, I was worshipping The Lord with songs on a music album. I was not consciously aware of anything in the Spirit realm. I was just normally going to eat my breakfast. As I was eating my prepared meal, Divine revelation *unexpectedly* erupted up in me.

*Suddenly*, I knew that Satan and the angels who followed him in rebellion against Living God have knowledge of how to procreate. I knew in certainty had they stayed in their Supreme God-ordained position and place for them, they could have used Holy knowledge for Good.

I knew with opened understanding that Holy God is unmistakably and astoundingly notifying all evil angels to their faces that they used His Holy Knowledge of procreating for their own selfish desires, and now He is stopping them. Supreme God is fully releasing Holy Knowledge to redeemed humankind on earth by informing them that He Created them with innate Creative ability to procreate with Him. He is divinely revealing to redeemed people that what they desire from the Holy intent in their hearts and so speak what they see from Visionary Glory is what procreates with Him in restoring the earth and the heavens back into Original Design. Procreation with Holy God comes through an established and ongoing relationship with Him.

**Legitimate Holy Procreating**

In the very beginning of Creation and time, God Supreme Sovereignly Created Adam in His very own Image and Likeness and endowed him with innate creative ability to procreate Good in the same way He does. Then He brought every living creature He Created to Adam to see what Adam would name them (Genesis 2:19–20a).

God of all Creation Created Lucifer as a Holy angel of Light, Knowledge, and Wisdom and also placed within him creative ability. But Lucifer betrayed His Creator and obstinately used his endowed free will to dishonor and pervert God's Holy Knowledge of Creativity. He misused this Holy Knowledge for his own selfish desires and as well persuaded other angels to join his coup against God's Kingdom of Righteousness.

By Lucifer's blatant self-centered rebellion, evil intent was illegally formulated. Lucifer chose to covet Creative Knowledge to use for his own selfish desire to promiscuously procreate to fulfill his evil lusts. He falsely and illegally set up an illegitimate kingdom of his own device. This was the origin of evil intent.

Then he slyly came into the Garden of Eden and duped humankind by saying, *...has God said!...* By these words, Lucifer was saying to Adam, *I also have knowledge of how to procreate from personal desires. If you listen to me and do as I say, you will be like God as I am*. Lucifer's perverse image of self-importance was already in his heart. He formulated unholy personal desires by perverting Holy knowledge God revealed to him in order to fit his own evil desires.

When you, who are Created and Designed in God's in Image and after His Likeness, receive God's redemption from evil by accepting His Son's innocent Blood Sacrifice that forgives all your sins and iniquities, you now live in Blood Covenant with Him. Therefore, you now have personal relationship with Creative God and can creatively formulate, frame, express, verbalize, voice, communicate, convey, devise, and invent your personal Holy plan that is good for you and for others. You together with others who have been redeemed by Jesus' Precious Blood Sacrifice can now creatively and visibly bring into existence the good you desire. Acting from your innate creativity completes God's Holy Plan for earth to exist in wholeness and productivity.

Indelibly implanted within each person is the creative ability to procreate with God. As each person communes with God in intimacy, He imparts within them His Holy Seed of creativity in freshness and newness. This is Holy and genuine procreation. From mutual intimate interaction with God, a Holy seed of innate creativity is deeply imparted within each person. This Holy seed of innate creativity is implanted within each person through their intimate communion with Holy God. Then what is implanted within them from procreating with Holy God is to be combined with the Holy Seed of creativity implanted within others who have procreated with Holy God.

The combining of people's creativity from procreating with Holy God works together for good to accomplish God's Perfect *Will* for earth and Heaven to flow in one complete Circle of Life. In Truth, Holy people procreating with Creative God and then joining together to manifest what they creatively procreate eliminates evil falseness by routing out all evil entities still vying to stay in charge as they see it. This process creates new heavens and new earth. Holy procreating replenishes the earth and restores what has been devastated by evil thus making a new earth where Righteousness dwells Eternally. This is how God's Righteous Kingdom is established on earth as it is in Heaven and how His *Will* is done on earth as it is in Highest Heaven so that one complete Circle of Life can flow unceasingly. This is the Way of Life for Eternity. When Heaven and earth are reconciled and restored as one complete operation as Holy God Originally Planned and Designed before the beginning of time, harmony reigns Eternally.

## Thoughts Are Doings

The Lord put on my heart to ask Him this question: "Do thoughts have sound waves?"

So I asked Him. *Suddenly*, understanding opened to me. I knew in the very essence of My being that existence is energy that emits sound waves, and these sound waves create whatever I think. Thoughts and sound waves are one and the same. Thoughts are sound waves that emanate Creative Energy which is the very Essence of Holy God whose Name is I AM WHO I AM. Creative Energy exists according to God's predetermined law or established principle of thermodynamics: the changing of a Living Substance from one form to another.

Humankind is Created in God's Holy Image and Likeness. Therefore, they have the same ability as He has to emit sound waves from thought intentions within the heart where decisions are formulated. I knew in unchangeable Truth what human beings think in their heart emits sound waves that creates good or evil...

You must know that creative ways of thinking are ingrained into the human psyche by a God who Created humankind in His Image and Likeness to be creative. Therefore, people emit sound waves that create whatever they are thinking in their heart—good or evil. God's laws of thermodynamics cannot be changed. Proactive God has given human beings a free-will to decide to selfishly create what benefits their egotistical agenda over the Good He wants for them. However, there are also people who choose to creatively create for good purposes for themselves and others.

When people declare aloud what they want to have happen in their environment, whether for good or for evil, what they speak is transmitted into the atmosphere around them as a decree. This decree of intention takes on an existence from what they speak from the thoughts in their heart.

The Holy Blood Jesus shed on The Cross redeems sinful mankind from perverted thinking. This is the only remedy that cleanses them from *all* unrighteousness. Supreme God created mankind to *think* good in their hearts and to creatively design good things for their enjoyment and God's Pleasure. As redeemed people rightfully think, they transmit sound waves that create good. God's Righteous thoughts are Holy doings that always create Good, not evil.

It must be recognized that both righteous thoughts and unrighteous thoughts that are transmitted into the atmosphere of the first and second heavens and into the earth are picked up and acted on either by those who have Holy Spirit living in them or by those who adhere to evil agendas.

Supreme God is presently disrupting evil in all its forms causing evil to bow to His Kingdom of Righteousness so that that evil cannot persist or continue. When those redeemed by Jesus' Blood Sacrifice declare aloud what they want to have happen in their environment that is for good, what they speak is transmitted into the atmosphere around them. Their righteous thoughts and spoken words against evil and for good notifies Satan and his hordes that they are being permanently judged.

The Lord reminded me of a recent instance in Walmart when I spoke healing to a young man being pushed in a wheelchair by his mother. Holy compassion rose up in me causing me to ask God to make him whole. However, there was no indication that He was made whole at that moment. As I pondered this encounter before The Lord, He instilled in me that to Him, it is always *now*, the present. God Eternal is not limited by time. What rises up in me to do from what He reveals to me in any situation I am in is accomplished in His Sight even though I may not see the things I pray, think, and speak being done in my time as I think they should be done. It is always *now* or in the present to Him even though to me on earth, it is yet future.

The Lord especially made me know that because the things I want to do are in my heart, I am doing them. This is how He sees it. Therefore, I emphatically knew that what I spoke from the righteous intentions in my heart healed this young man and made him whole. God marked him healed and made whole by the inaudible words I spoke that were in my heart. My Holy thoughts are sound waves that create what I think in my heart even though they are not spoken aloud. God hears these thoughts that are Living words to Him, and He Acts on these Holy inaudible words. This is Eternal Life in action.

I know the thoughts in my heart are doings and emanate from an upright heart that has been cleansed through Jesus' Blood Sacrifice; therefore, I have the assurance that the good things I think are performed. My Holy thoughts emit sound waves and bring into being the good desire that is my heart through the words I speak and the actions I take. This is operating in Eternal Ways. Only the Pure in heart see God in Eternal Ways. When our hearts are Pure, we do Eternal things that are good and transmit sound waves that formulate the good intention in our heart.

## God's Mesh of Communication Wires

God has communication wires that glow as Pure white Glory Light. These Glory Light communication wires cannot be separated. They are intertwined and work together into one complete message no matter when they are spoken—times past, times present, or times yet to come.

At this time of polluted thinking and words, there is a mesh of unholy communication wires that are hindering God's mesh of Glory Light communication wires from fully operating as He Originally Designed.

God's Glory Light mesh of communication wires are being confiscated by complacency and acceptance of polluted communication wires that operate through compromise. When emphatic action is taken against this polluted mesh of wires, God's flow of Power and Energy causes Creative Action that annihilates the polluted mesh of wires.

Continuously plugging into God's communication wires of Glory Light through praise and worship to Him ignites His Energy and Power to flow causing action to occur. What you think and speak creates your desired intent. Thoughts are doings, and so are words of action. Holy God is I AM WHO I AM. He is always present and continuously in motion or action. I AM is perpetual Power and Energy that flows and never ceases and so causes Action whether or not this Power and Energy is acknowledged or accepted by His Creations. This is why there is no cessation of existence. Perpetual Energy continuously Creates whatever is thought or spoken.

Thank You, Lord. I choose to continuously plug myself into Your communication wires of Glory Light Energy and Power. Therefore, I am Blessed indeed to walk in the Holy capacity of Your communication wires that create action that gives You all the Glory. I trust you to keep me in Your Higher Way of living on earth that establishes Your Righteous Kingdom in the heavens and on the earth. May my thoughts and words always Create action. So be it, Lord!

## Creative Glory Acts

Through Holy Divine encounters, Holy Spirit is teaching me how to supernaturally transport from the material realm into the invisible realm to accomplish The Lord's Holy Purposes. Being supernaturally transported means to vanish in the natural flow on earth to flow with Holy Spirit by being supernaturally transferred from one place to another in order to minister Holy God's Purpose into the situation for which He wants to manifest Himself to bring His Light of Life and Love.

These Holy encounters do not derive from New Age philosophy of astral transport. New Age teachers have tapped into this truth of Holy Spirit transportation and so are using legitimate Holy Spirit Ways for illegitimate and unholy purposes. God's infallible Laws He instituted to maintain His Creation cannot be changed. However, God's Laws that He indelibly established to govern His Creation can be thwarted and used for evil purposes.

There are those who have tapped into God's indelible Laws to selfishly promote themselves for monetary gain, fame, and power. New Age philosophy that is being publicly disseminated and transmitted is another form of deception. Deception is twisted truth portrayed as legitimate. Deception is truth intertwined and wrapped in lies. Satan is a master of deception. He is a liar and a deceiver. The Lord wants those who may be deceitfully using illegitimate power to turn to Him so they come out of darkness into His Marvelous Light and use His legitimate Laws of Power for good rather than for selfish purposes. Satan is a deceiver and a liar who makes himself appear as Light and Power attracting those who do not know Truth to fall prey to his wiles. Jesus Christ is the only Way, Truth, and Life that human beings should live by (2 Corinthians 11:13–14).

In John's Gospel, chapter 8:44–45 in the Holy Bible, Jesus emphatically exposes Satan as a deceiver and a liar:

*For you are the children of your father the devil, and you love to do the evil things he does. He was a murderer from the beginning. He has always hated the truth, because there is no truth in him. When he lies, it is consistent with his character; for he is a liar and the father of lies. So when I* [Jesus] *tell the truth, you just naturally don't believe Me!*

Supernatural transportation is being legitimately transferred by Holy Spirit to a specific location to minister for The Lord in helping someone in distress they cannot get free from or to answer the questions in their hearts that they are asking. There are documented accounts in The Holy Bible of God answering the cry of someone's heart by supernaturally sending His servants to them. Read some recorded accounts in 1 Kings 18:10–12, 2 Kings 4:1–7, John 2:1–11, and in Acts 8:26–40; 16:6-10. There are as well other recorded accounts in The Holy Bible of supernatural operations to meet people's desperate needs that override the human spirit and demonic influence to accomplish Holy God's *Will*.

I said, "Lord, I am traveling on a road less traveled. I know factually that I am walking properly in Holy relationship with You. Therefore, I want to know Truth concerning how to be supernaturally transported to carry out Your *Will* on earth and in the heavens. How do I discern where to walk into this supernatural transportation point and so be taken where You want me to be to minister Your Word of Truth? Where is this supernatural transportation point for me? Do You want me to come into a higher level of this? If so, I want to be used by You to meet people's profound and deepest needs. How am I to do this? I ask You, Lord, to bring me into a higher level of discernment to learn how to mystically transport into situations to accomplish a Holy Purpose You have for taking me into situations to meet the need in a circumstance to accomplish Your *Will*. Reveal more to me that I do not yet understand so I can move to a higher level of discernment in being supernaturally transported to cooperate with You in accomplishing Your *Will* and Holy Purposes for what is needed in a situation. Thank You."

As I surrendered my will to The Lord, He opened understanding to me and answered me. He opened comprehension to discern Truth in knowing that I am to submit to His *Will* in each encounter He takes me into. He revealed to me that there are different levels of being supernaturally transported just as there are differing levels of maturity.

The Lord made me to know that I am supernaturally transported into situations within the dreams and visions that occur in the Spirit realm. He also revealed to me that supernatural occurrences happen in my circumstances in the natural realm of this world. Nevertheless, these are both supernatural encounters bringing God's Life of Truth into the situation where I find myself either in my dreams and visions in the Spirit realm or in my natural circumstances.

He let me know that when I am taken into situations by Holy Spirit in dreams or visions or in the natural, these encounters are actually occurring for the purpose of bringing His Truth into a situation. When He transports me into a circumstance in dreams or visions, it is for the purpose of carrying out His *Will* in a circumstance so His Purpose is accomplished without interference from the demonic realm or human souls thinking their own thoughts.

I know emphatically by Holy Spirit that these Holy encounters will continue and that I am to allow Him to use me in this way so His Holy *Will* is accomplished in the situations He transports me into for His Holy Purposes to be accomplished in each situation He takes me into.

I responded, "Yes, Lord! As You have spoken to me, let it be done for me. I am willing to be transported in whatever way You choose to send me to accomplish a good work in the place you take me. I don't hesitate to tell You I do not understand in fullness all You have spoken to Me concerning Spiritual journeying for Your Purposes. Keep me from supposing I know when I really don't know how to obey You to carry out what You are revealing to me. Impress in me to ask You what I need to know. Thank You!"

**Personal Holy Supernatural Encounters**

As directed by The Lord, I have been concentrating on being transported by Holy Spirit to accomplish God's *Will* in bringing Heaven to earth. I know that these Holy encounters from The Lord have happened to me on occasion over the years. Yet I am sensing there is more The Lord wants for me to accomplish in this area because The Lord spoke to me that there are different levels of being transported into situations that I need to know and experience to accomplish His *Will*.

The Lord instilled deep with me that every time I pray, I am being transported and taken on the scene to transform the situation from darkness to Light. I understand that when I come on the scene through my prayers, I see by Holy Spirit what to ask and then declare. Thus, I know how to pray in every situation that arises. When I open my mouth and speak, Holy Spirit instantly transports me into the situation as if I was presently in the situation. I know that the more I pray, the more my words are being transferred into the place God is taking them to change the circumstances for good.

By Holy Spirit Operations, Heaven and earth are linked in cooperation to fulfill all Righteousness in accomplishing One Eternal Circle of Life as Supreme God Originally Designed. Therefore, Satan cannot interrupt this Flow or these Holy maneuvers (planned and controlled movement, skillful strategy, or scheme—secret plan, an orderly combination of things on a definite plan).

Speaking words, which is praying, transfers you into the situations of your choosing. You can freely pick and choose the scenarios you want to become a part of in prayer declarations. Other times, Holy God chooses where He wants to take you to accomplish a Unique Purpose He has in a particular situation. Holy angels transport your words into the situation to bring Light that dispels darkness.

Holy angel messengers take the words you speak or declare in prayer and imprint these words on the hearts of humankind who are refusing Holy God in these very last days of time on earth. This is happening so people know the Truth of God's Word and so are without excuse. God's Words you declare in prayer are forcing people to accept or reject the Holy words you speak. God's Holy angels are taking these words and imprinting them in their hearts. No person will speak to them, but the Holy words spoken are taken by God's Holy angels and imprinted on rebellious hearts, and these words alone will speak to people so they have no excuse before God. Every person will have heard of Supreme God, and they will know it. No one can excuse themselves before Holy God at the time He calls every person to give an account of their lives to Him (Romans 1:18–32, Jeremiah 17:10, Revelation 2:23).

Holy God's spoken Word is alive and active and working and always Lives before Him in the atmosphere. Thoughts are spoken words. So words either thought or spoken do not desist or return void or empty of fulfillment (Isaiah 55:11). God's Word does a work of dividing and separating the thoughts and the intents within the hearts of people (Hebrews 4:12–13). If people say they have never heard God's Word, it is because they refuse to hear and give heed to His Word spoken to them or imprinted on their hearts Romans (1:18–32).

As I continuously yield to The Lord, I increase in learning how to supernaturally transport into a higher level to accomplish God's Holy purposes. The Lord is making known to me that there is so much more He wants to do in the realm of the supernatural with my cooperation which seems to me to be supernatural but to God is the only Way He interchanges.

I follow Righteous Protocol in going back and forth from the natural realm to the supernatural realm by saying, "Through the Blood of Jesus on the Mercy Seat, I have Legal Authority to go into the spiritual realm and then come back into the natural realm. I stand in My Righteous Authority through The Blood of Jesus interceding on the Mercy Seat, and I step forward into the spiritual realm as an act of my will. Through Jesus' Faith that dwells in me, I give The Lord permission to take me where He wants to use me for His Glory and someone else's good. I as well give myself permission to supernaturally transport through time and space to accomplish The Lord's Holy *Will* in the circumstance for which He is transporting me."

God chooses when and how to supernaturally transport us where He wants to use us to release His Word and Love and Power into situations. When we step into the spirit realm through the Blood of Jesus, we wait on The Lord to see where He wants to take us to accomplish His *Will* in the situation. Supernatural encounters may or may not be immediate. They may occur in dreams and visions during the night or during the daytime. Supernatural encounters can happen in earth's natural circumstances that we are naturally part of or He sends us into. When we obey Holy Spirit's directions in the situations, the supernatural encounter is completed. Then we step back into the natural realm knowing that God's *Will* was accomplished by our obedience in allowing Him to supernaturally transport us into situations as He so chooses.

**Holy Spirit Adventures**

I was obeying Holy Spirit operations by command of The Lord to not fear to do what He is asking me to do because it won't look like what I have been doing. He let me know that I am to trust Him in taking me to places through Spiritual journeying for His Purposes of halting evil entities in their tracks who are defying Him and attempting to steal His Creation for their own pleasure. He revealed to me that He is God of Might and Power and that He is no longer allowing evil entities to defy Him. As I submit my will to obey Him in doing His *Will His Way*, He is operating Glory Fire Power through me to annihilate all evil entities who are vying for illegitimate Power control over His creations.

The Lord is now using people fully committed to doing His *Will* His Way to bring an end to all those who are vying for illicit power control. He let me know that by my trust in Him, He is taking me places by transporting me into a situation to speak for Him. This is a Spiritual journey, not a natural physical journey on earth.

I knew emphatically that I was to let go of myself and hold on to The Lord as a matter of total surrender. This was not a matter of my doing anything, but a willing surrender of myself to The Lord by sanctified trust. Then I felt a heaviness and sleepiness while attempting to do housework. I could not shake this or go on doing what I was doing.

I knew I was to stop what I was doing and just sit down and take a nap. The Lord let me know that this sleepiness was from Him. I obeyed what I was feeling and sat down and took a nap. Later, The Lord revealed to me that because I obeyed Him in taking a nap, He saw my obedience as preparation to be taken into Holy Spirit encounters for His Purposes, and He would be expanding me and taking me places in the Spirit realm to do a Holy work needed in the situation.

## Personal Supernatural Encounter

I awoke this morning from a reality encounter in the Spirit realm that was still vividly alive in me. As I was waking up, these words reverberated all through me, *I see this man, and I am pleased with him.* I saw myself walking down the corridor of a hospital and walking into someone's hospital room. I saw this person's family was there, and they were weeping because of this person's sickness that seemed to be unto death. It became crystal clear to me that I was to speak these words over this person, and I did: *"This sickness is not unto death. It is for the Glory of God to be seen. This is another opportunity for your family and other people to believe in Jesus as Savior and Lord."*

When I was fully awake, I got up and went to my Prayer Room for the purpose of coming into the Council of the Godly as He has mandated I do often. I drew near to Almighty God approaching Him through The Holy Blood of Jesus which is the appropriate and proper protocol to come into His Presence and into the Council of the Godly. I worshipped The Lord by giving Him Praise and Thanksgiving to honor Him. Then I picked up my Bible and began my daily Bible reading in the Gospel of John. I began reading in John chapter 9 and read through chapter 11. *Suddenly*, the words Jesus spoke in John 11:4 and then verse 15 rose up in me and became so alive in me:

*"Lazarus' sickness will not end in death. No, it is for the glory of God. I, the Son of God, will receive glory from this. Lazarus is dead. And for your sake, I am glad I wasn't there, because this will give you another opportunity to believe in Me. Come, let's go see him."*

I then put these words together with the account I read in John 9 of the man who was born blind being healed by Jesus and Jesus saying that this man being born blind was for the Glory of God to be seen.

While still pondering Jesus' words in John's Gospel, The Lord led me to 1 Kings 17 to the story of Elijah raising the widow's son from death and the woman saying to Elijah, *"Now I know for sure that you are a man of God, and that the Lord truly speaks through you."*

Instantly, I knew that these words I spoke to this man and his family was for The Lord's Glory to be seen so this man, his family, and other people would be given another opportunity to believe in Jesus as Savior and Lord.

*Suddenly*, I recognized this supernatural encounter concerned an actual personal situation happening in a family, one of whom, I was ministering God's Love and Truth. Their loved one was suffering from post-traumatic syndrome from being in war zones. I shared this with the one person in this family to whom I have been ministering God's Love for this entire family. I shared with this person that the suffering man's immediate family was to speak these words over their loved one. She said she would relay this to them. I knew in actuality from our conversations that I would not be accepted by this entire family if I were physically on the scene with them. Therefore, I literally saw and knew in reality that God was working in this family's circumstances to fulfill His Word to them because of our agreed prayers for this situation.

I realized the Scriptures I read in John 9 and 11 along with 1 Kings 17 focused on God's Glory. I saw in truth The Lord was answering what I asked Him recently from the Words that so powerfully rose up in me to ask Him, "Transpose me, Lord, into a higher realm of Glory Influence in both supernatural and natural Holy encounters to accomplish Your Purposes. Thank You."

The Lord let me know I created an atmosphere of Glory Influence when I obeyed speaking His Words He gave me to speak in this supernatural encounter where He placed me. My obedience allowed Holy Spirit operations to manifest to help these people in their dire situation. To God alone be all the Glory and thanksgiving.

**Steering Wheels—Magnetic Force**

During the night, I found myself in another reality encounter I did not fully understand. I was holding on to a large steering wheel and flying through the air being taken to places. I could feel the sensation of a very strong magnetic force in my body pulling me through the air causing me to fly around and go to places as I held tightly to the steering wheel. I could not pull away from this strong magnetic force nor could I let go of the large wheel or stop myself from flying. I was laughing with glee and thoroughly enjoying this very strong magnetic force that was pulling me around and taking me places as I held tightly to the steering wheel. I wanted to keep doing this and didn't want it to stop.

While I was flying at whirlwind speed, I looked to my right to see where I was going and what was around me. I saw what seemed to me to be an angel with long flowing hair streaked with subdued colors of emerald green, silvery blue-gray, and brilliant white. Yet I saw me holding onto this steering wheel and flying through space at a whirlwind pace being taken to places by this strong magnetic force. I couldn't determine if the angel was the magnetic force or if the angel was carrying me even though I was holding the steering wheel. This angel was laughing with glee and enjoying this flight. As I was flying through the air, I kept seeing that the steering wheel had a straight cross bar in the middle at a right angle. I didn't understand this.

Eventually I came back down to earth and as I stood there, I saw standing side by side a small-sized steering wheel and a large-sized steering wheel. The small-sized wheel looked exactly like the large wheel. Both were perfectly round circles that had soft comfortable suede-like padding with tiny holes in the suede material, but the large steering wheel had a bar in the middle that was at a right angle going from southwest to northeast. The small steering wheel was a clear circle with no bar in the middle. I looked at this wondering what it meant. I didn't know why I was seeing side by side a small steering wheel and a large steering wheel that had a right angle crossbar that was not in the small steering wheel.

I knew I could take hold of the small-sized steering wheel that looked just like the large steering wheel minus the right angle crossbar. I did take hold of the small wheel, but nothing happened. I just stood there holding the small steering wheel. There was no force or power. So I let go of the small wheel and took hold of the large wheel. As soon as I took hold of the large wheel, I was instantly pulled by a great magnetic force and was again flying through the air going places.

Later, as I was pondering this, I instinctively knew that I could take whichever steering wheel I wanted—the small or the large. I knew the small wheel was the way I wanted to go. I knew that large steering wheel was greater than the small-sized steering wheel and would take me where

I could not go myself. I knew as well that I could not go the way I wanted to go if I took hold of the large wheel.

I deeply pondered what the bar at a right angle inside the large steering wheel going from southwest to northeast meant. The Spirit of God rose up in me. Instantly, I knew that the bar in the middle of the large wheel gives strength to the circle or steering wheel. I knew that the bar going from southwest to northeast represents that I am looking from the earth up to God in Heaven, and this is what causes a magnetic force that works in cooperation with God and gives me strength in taking me where I cannot go myself. Because it is at a right angle means that I am doing things the *right way*, which is God's Way. This is what causes the magnetic force to take me to the places where God can work His Purposes in the situation.

God is making known that He wants to burst through and break off the bondages in people's lives. People are drawn as a magnet to those who are totally free from the effect of evil all around them. Those who carry Glory Fire Presence speak Holy words that draw people to hear what they speak. Therefore, they are not to withdraw or pull back from speaking God's Holy Word. Holy Glory Fire Presence emanates through holy words of decree spoken and creative actions performed. This is what burns constraints so bridges can be built between God and people. Speaking from Glory Fire Presence allows a River of Life to flow through those who allow God to flow through them as He *Wills*. As God flows through those who allow Him to, God's Holy angels show up and listen and go to perform the words spoken by their mouths.

These words rose up in my spirit: **Don't consider and Go! Just Go and Flow! In the Flow is the Know!**

The Lord is revealing that people are not to consider how to go or go doing what they consider to do or do what has always been done. Each one is to go flowing with God in The River of Life and Truth so intuitively they know *when* to go, *where* to go, and *what to do and say* in every situation they find themselves.

Declare over yourself continuously: **I will always be in the right place, at the right time, with the right word, among the right people!**

Wow! Lord! What secret things you reveal to me. I love You.

### Pure Worship Creates Glory Substance

In a dream, I was in a place among people observing them. I was mulling over what I observed happening among these people. A misty substance or cloud emerged and floated by me flowing or floating around in this place among the people. I watched people being healed, delivered, and set free. They were instantly transformed and brought out of darkness that enabled them to see Light.

Then, I saw the same rectangle Box I previously saw at a distance coming down from Heaven. However, now it was close at hand in the place where I was. Instantly, I recognized the Visionary Glory Box was carrying Visionary Glory, which are words to say and, actions to do for the need at hand. I knew that I was to open this Visionary Glory Box to see how to operate Glory Influence.

At this point, the dream ended, and I was awake. I emphatically knew that from now on, I am to open this Visionary Glory Box containing Visionary Glory in every situation or circumstance The Lord places me or takes me whether in the invisible realm or in the visible realm.

I intuitively knew that worshipping and praising God creates Glory Substance. Pure and Holy vessels offering Pure worship to God brings His Glory Fire Influence on the scene bringing Light that eliminates every form of darkness. Darkness is evil that has a form that causes sickness and death. Glory Fire Influence brings God's Substance of Life in the form of Light that eradicates darkness.

At the moment people see Light, they truly understand Truth, and they choose God, The Light of Life. When they choose Holy God, the darkness in them is immediately transformed into Light, and they are changed from darkness to Light causing them to be free and come out of darkness into His Holy Light. This is why there is always Holy mist surrounding God. Only Purity and Holiness Creates Glory Substance. When Holy Mist, which is Glory Substance, comes into a situation, darkness flees, and people are healed, delivered, and set free.

Redeemed people, who live Holy lives and who are obedient to God, have the innate ability to cause Glory Mist to manifest around them. This Glory mist may or may not be visible, but rest assured it is present. Glory mist flows into situations when redeemed people give Holy God, their Creator, Pure and Holy worship. God gladly receives this Pure worship to Him. Pure worship expressed in praise creates a Holy Mist, which is the Substance of Life. The Substance of Life brings Glory Fire Influence that manifests a molecular change in the atmosphere and so restructures darkness to become Light. From God's Light or Holy Mist emanates the Substance of Life causing creative happenings. From the invisible Visionary Glory Substance of Life, actual material objects can be creatively formed and brought into visible and tangible substance on earth by specific words of decree spoken and creative acts performed that bring into material existence human body parts, water, food, gold, spheres of dominion, and creative miracles of all kinds in many forms.

Spoken words cause quantum physics to activate transforming the invisible Substance of Life back into its Original form of Light bringing molecular change into visible matter that can be used on earth as Originally Designed and Created by Holy God.

Pure and Holy worship to Holy God creates quantum mechanics that causes living frequencies to vibrate with Life-giving Energy. Only Holy and Pure worship to Creative God creates Light that transforms the invisible Substance of Life into tangible matter that turns the darkness of evil back into Light in original form.

This occurs when God's Created Holy angels and Blood-redeemed people Created in God's Image and Likeness offer Him Pure and Holy worship. This combined Pure worship to Him causes the Creative Substance of Life to manifest into material matter which appears to human beings living in the material realm as Creative Miracles but is Almighty God's only Way of Life. When mist or clouds of Light known as Shekinah Glory Influence comes into a situation, God's Holiness manifests and eradicates the darkness of evil in all its forms and brings Light that Creates.

Thank You, Holy God, for Holy Revelation Truth. Increase our ability to offer You Pure and Holy worship so that through our obedience to flow in Glory Fire Influence operations as led by Holy Spirit, evil is eradicated, and the earth and the heavens are transformed back into Original forms of Light which establishes Your Holy Kingdom of Righteousness that Reigns for Eternity.

## Transporting Visionary Glory

In a dream, I saw myself pushing a grocery cart. I saw this over and over. I also saw others around me pushing grocery carts.

The Lord instructed me to know that His redeemed people are transporting Visionary Glory Influence everywhere they go. Visionary Glory operates when you are around people in the circumstances where God places you or where you go by choice or are invited. Visionary Glory does not operate in isolation. You carry God's Presence into your personal situation. Redeemed people carry Holy God's Presence that creates an atmosphere of Glory Fire Influence all around them in their circumstance that tangibly removes all that is not of Him. Each redeemed person bringing God's Holy Presence into a situation must remember to open the Visionary Glory Box carrying Visionary Glory Influence and then speak or act from what you see or hear from Visionary Glory Influence. When this is done, Glory Fire Influence carries your spoken words of decree and creatively designed actions into your current situation or circumstance and brings lasting change for Good.

Visionary Glory is transported into your present circumstance by the Holy Creative words you speak, the visions or pictures you see that show you prayer to verbalize, specific healing pronouncements, a Blessing or a Righteous judgement to decree. Know that **Glory Influence Flows out of your body, shines on your face, and transports through your smile, and manifests through your words**.

I cried out to The Lord, "Lord, why are there times when I don't see immediate visible manifestations when I speak? I know and truly believe that the Substance of Life exists in the invisible realm in a form that manifests into visible matter by the words I speak?"

The Lord let me know that when I speak, my Holy and Anointed words cause manifestations that I may or may not see. No matter what is happening around me, I am to keep my focus on Him, not on whether or not I see immediate manifestations. The Lord is revealing that Visionary Glory operations are launching the new heavens and new earth to replace the devastation from evil. Visionary Glory is bringing into manifestation Eternal Living.

**Unused Words in Visionary Glory Box**

The Lord openly revealed to me that there are still unused words in this Visionary Glory Box that are to be spoken to create what is needed on earth during the time Satan is attempting to shut down Holy God's Creative Ways of Living for Good.

My spirit was greatly stirred to know more about these unused words. So in all boldness I asked The Lord to reveal more to me concerning the unused words in this Visionary Glory Box that I instinctively recognize need to be spoken so they create and bring into manifestation what is needed on earth when Satan is attempting to shut down what God Created for Good and evil is blatantly being flaunted.

These words rose up in me to declare: "In Jesus' Name and by the Power of Holy Spirit, I release the Glory Influence to displace and stop the powers of darkness that would halt any request I decree. Amen! Glory be to You, O Lord God Most High!"

Intuitively, I knew that the unspoken and inaudible Holy Words contained in the Visionary Glory Box are being spoken by Supreme God. I strongly sense in my spirit that Almighty God is releasing these unused words contained in the Visionary Glory Box. I knew by revelation knowledge rising in me that these unused Words are not being heard by human or demonic hearing. Nevertheless, these unused words are underway and are actually happening without the devil's or people's knowledge so that Holy God's Will for heaven and earth to be reconciled together as one operation is not thwarted.

Supreme God is soundlessly speaking unspoken Holy Words contained in the Visionary Glory Box. These unused words being spoken by Holy God release Shekinah Glory Power that is causing *sudden* destruction bringing to an end all things as they are now so that the new heavens and the new earth can be established by the Visionary Glory operations being spoken into material existence by God's redeemed people.

**Religious Spirit and Human Will Join**

The Lord is issuing a warning to all those pursuing to learn Holy Supernatural Ways of Eternal existence that they are to be fully aware that the unsanctified human will and the religious spirit are uniting and working together. These unholy spirits are presently increasing their combined operations to work in unison to shut down Holy Glory Fire operations flowing through all of those carrying Glory Fire Influence by the Power and Life of Holy Spirit.

The Lord is warning that this will happen through people we presently trust or have formerly trusted by association who, for whatever reason, allow unholy spirits to influence them. Subtle deception is at work in a greater degree and manner trying to get those carrying Holy Glory Fire Influence off target. Casual trust can no longer be accepted by immaturity and blind acceptance.

The human will can be transformed by the religious spirit operating under the radar undetected. Its deceitful maneuvers ensnare unsuspecting people who just go to church to look acceptable to others and yet truly believe they are acceptable to God. The unholy operations of the religious spirit are altering the rational thinking of many people and so are holding them captive to a form of religion without Holy Power manifestations because they do not know The Lord on Holy intimate terms.

To those who do not detect this joint operation between the unsanctified human will and the religious spirit, the power of this unholy alliance is increasingly deceiving those *playing church* which keeps them entwined in half-truth and half lies.

Alert discernment wrapped in Holy Love must operate in those carrying Glory Fire Presence enabling them to detect unholy operations deceitfully working in people who are not awake and watching. Those carrying Glory Fire Influence are to adhere to God's Holy Word when they are around suspicious people so as not to fall prey to deceiving ways that pulls unsuspecting people into its web. Absorb and heed God's Word in Romans 16:17-20, Hebrews 13:9a, Ephesians 5:6-11, Colossians 2:8, 2 Timothy 3:1-9, Luke 21:8, Matthew 24:4-12.

An increased number of people walking in Glory Fire Influence are being sent by The Lord to come on the scene in Power demonstrations. This causes the religious spirit and the human will to become stirred and unsettled causing them to increase their joint effort to stay in charge of church operations as they see it.

At this point of delusion, deceived people who are so ingrained in deception openly accept the half-truth and half-lies from this unholy alliance as Truth. So they see no need to repent because they sincerely, although wrongly, believe they are fine. They mistakenly and confidently believe that those walking in Glory Fire Influence are in deception; therefore, they have the unmitigated right to turn and attack those walking in Glory Fire Influence. Those who allow themselves to be held captive to deception will betray those who are powerfully carrying Glory Fire influence.

Jesus warned that those doing this will think they are doing God a favor:

*I have said all this to you, to keep you from falling away. They will put you out of the synagogues; indeed, the hour is coming when whoever kills you will think he is offering service to God.* (John 16:1–2)

*They went out from us, but they were not of us; for if they had been of us, they would have continued with us; but they went out, that it might be plain that they all are not of us.* (1 John 2:19)

This is why those who are walking in Glory Fire Power must remain alert in every area of their lives. Deception is no respecter of persons. Its ploy is for all people. It is imperative to stay alert by walking in Truth as recorded in

The Holy Bible. Pure worship to Holy God from an undefiled heart washed clean by The Blood of Jesus keeps you alert to all forms of pride and deception.

In a dream, I was with another Holy woman of God who ministers The Lord's Life and Truth wherever she goes alone or we go together as He leads us. In this dream, we were together watching an old lady sitting on a low stool fixing a bicycle rim or tire.

I saw us saying to her, "We will pay you."

She said, "I don't want you to pay me."

We said, "We want to pay you. You deserve to be paid."

She kept saying, "I don't want to get paid."

We kept on talking with her.

She adamantly said, "I don't want to hear what you are saying."

*Suddenly*, I saw in such vivid vibrant colors teams of horses go by me. There were six horses to a team. They were in full speed ahead, seemingly flying past me. They caught my attention. I felt like I wanted to go after them. They appeared to be pulling stagecoaches full of people one after another. I saw many, many activities like you would see at a Country Fair all going on at the same time, and this scene was so vibrantly alive and in full vibrant colors. I so wanted to be part of this. I felt so very, very happy. I didn't want what I was seeing to ever end.

I said, "I am going after the horses. I love horses, and I am going after them." So I got in my car and headed after the horses which I could see in the far distance. They went so fast I couldn't catch them. So I stopped going after them and turned around in a driveway to return to where I was. I recall the driveway was not a straight driveway but completely rounding in front of a beautiful architecturally-designed house. The rounding patio-looking driveway was made of pretty pinkish textured of bricks of smooth yet imprinted design. As I turned around to leave the textured driveway, I saw the yard had lush green grass and was well-manicured. Vibrantly beautiful flowers lined the driveway and were closely aligned along the driveway where I was turning around to head back to where I was. I was looking out my window watching the driveway trying to stay on the driveway so as not to smash the vibrant flowers or get in the beautifully-manicured yard. I was captured by the beauty of this driveway and how closely it was aligned with the vibrantly-alive grass and flowers. I didn't know why I was so particularly drawn to these. I just was. So much so that I was looking down at them from my driver's window to make sure I did not drive over them as I was turning around to leave the driveway.

Next, I was back again with my ministry friend. We were again in the presence of the old lady fixing the bicycle.

We said to her, "We know! You don't want to be paid."

She said, "Now I do. I want to hear what you are saying."

We said, "We don't have anything to tell you."

I was puzzled by the old lady formerly not wanting to hear and now wanting to hear what we had to say and our saying we don't have anything to tell you. I pondered this dream for days. I almost dismissed it because I did not understand it.

Then The Lord opened my understanding. I perceived in my spirit that this old lady's reaction was the typical reply that the unsanctified human will that is aligned with the religious spirit speaks. They want to hear on their own terms when they want to hear. Then when they decide they want to hear, The Lord doesn't have anything to say to them. They missed His timing in what He wanted to say to them. The happy times are going on without them. They can't join in the happy times that are happening at a fast pace because they didn't want to hear what The Lord wanted to personally speak to them when He came to them individually or through others He sent to them with His Glory Fire Influence to make Himself known to them as He wants to be known. His Holy Desire is for them to turn to Him with all their hearts (Mark 12:30–31).

I also see that if we who are speaking to others what The Lord is saying also do not get on board with the fast-paced activities The Lord is doing at this time, we too will get left behind to do our own thing.

**Religious Spirit Rendered Powerless**

The religious spirit aligned with the unsanctified human will attacks Glory Fire Operations. Jesus was publicly shut down so many times by the religious spirit operating through unsanctified human wills. At this time on earth, the Authority of Jesus is being released and carried out through His redeemed people who carry His Glory Fire Influence by being obedient to do...*the greater works...* of Power and Glory that Jesus said we would do after He ascended back to His Father (John 14:12). Those who are obedient to do...*the greater works*...are causing the religious spirit to be shut down in all its forms through their Holy Glory Fire operations being carried out under the guidance of Holy Spirit.

Through a Holy and uniquely orchestrated assignment, The Lord came upon me mightily. Spirit tongues flowed through me all day long. This was an unusual day. I knew Glory Fire operations were being performed in cooperation with Holy God. I let these Holy Spirit operations flow into me and out through me. The Power and Presence of The Lord Almighty was evidently on me the entire day. I just flowed with His directions. Travailing, groaning prayer fell on me as Fire. I could not stop this nor did I want to. The Lord revealed to me that this was His Glory Fire operating through me to render the religious spirit inoperative and unable to keep God's fully committed people captive and in bondage to its illicit tactics.

Holy Glory Fire operations continued through me and intensified in cooperation with my friend The Lord brought into my life to walk alongside me in ministry. Even though we were not physically together at this time, we kept in contact by texts to each other. I was keeping her updated on what The Lord was doing through me that was bringing the religious spirit's stronghold of illegal influence into subjection to God's Holy Authority so God's redeemed people are released from lies and deception. The Lord arranged our circumstances so we would come into Holy agreement with each other and with Him in rendering the religious spirit permanently powerless to operate in any form. We joined our hearts and words together in Holy agreement. In the mouth of two or three witnesses shall every word be established (Deuteronomy 19:15, 2 Corinthians 13:1).

These Spirit-led actions are part of...*the greater works*... Jesus said we would be doing when He returned to sit at His Father's Right Hand and sent us Holy Spirit (John 14:12–14).

During the night as I lay in my bed, I was rehearsing the Glory Fire operations against the religious spirit that The Lord did through me today in agreement with my Holy friend. I heard myself asking The Lord, "Is the religious spirit now rendered powerless by the Mighty Acts You did through me against this ugly spirit and in agreement with You and my Holy friend, or are we to continue bombarding the religious spirit to stop it from operating?"

A clean and Pure fragrance permeated my room as I lay on my bed. I knew it was the sweet fragrance of Heaven being released. I deeply breathed in this sweet and Pure fragrance. I kept doing this. I could not get enough of this smell.

I indelibly knew that the fragrance of Heaven is now released to encompass God's redeemed people. Therefore, they are now free to follow Him **if** they so choose. People can no longer be held captive by religious spirit ways unless they choose to stay complacent to its wiles. God's Holy operations have set people free to see and hear Holy God's Voice above the clamor of the religious spirit. Therefore, even more of...*the greater works*... Jesus declared His disciples would do can come forth through them.

Through the obedient actions of my friend working in cooperation with me in obedience to The Lord's directions, God's Holy anger was unleashed and His Holy Wrath spent on this religious spirit who has held His people captive by strangulation so they could not see or hear Him. Now those who choose to comply with Holy Spirit's direction are free from the entanglement of the religious spirit. They can accurately know The Lord in Truth and openly experience His Love for them in going forth doing...*the greater works*...they now have the uninterrupted ability to carry out.

If people receive what The Lord is openly revealing concerning the religious spirit being permanently rendered powerless, they are fully released to follow Him and as well to operate...*the greater works*...as Jesus said we would. Count on this: no more unsanctified human will and religious spirit operating together to keep God's people captive to lies and deception.

The religious spirit has been dealt a powerful blow that restrains its unholy actions against God's Holy people causing all the redeemed in Heaven and on earth to rejoice together. No longer can people excuse themselves nor can they blame God for their selfish decisions. Only those filled with Holy Spirit who receive what has been accomplished against the religious spirit will agree with God and so flow in this Holy knowledge.

The Lord made it evidently clear to me that everywhere God's redeemed people go, we are to declare the religious spirit powerless to operate. We are to forbid this religious spirit to lie and deceive us. Each redeemed person is to emphatically state to this religious spirit that it no longer has any power to operate its lies and deception to keep God's Holy people captive to its evil lies. We are to continually remind this religious spirit that it has been permanently dismantled by declaring loudly and openly with bold Authority:

**Supreme God and I have come into agreement against you, religious spirit. I legally demand you**

**by the Authority of Almighty God to let God's people go! You no longer have any power to lie and deceive or strangle God's people! Says The Lord, "Let My people go!"**

The religious spirit has been dealt a powerful blow and has been rendered permanently powerless by the obedience to Holy Spirit-led operations.

All Glory, Power, and Dominion is Yours, Supreme God of Creation. I know in Truth that agreeing with You in unified agreement renders the religious spirit powerless in all its forms and so seals on earth and in the heavens Your Kingdom of Righteousness and Justice. Praise be to Almighty God forever and ever! AMEN!

Hallelujah! Amen and Amen multiplied many times over!

**Church Leaders and Religious Spirit**

However, the religious spirit is still active in organized churches because there are those who worship God with their lips while their hearts are far from Him. In doing this, they hold the form of religion, but they deny God's Power to work Truth in them because they allow their human will to override God's Word. When the religious spirit aligns with a strong human will, a powerful alliance is formed causing deception to operate unleashed. People who are in captivity to the spirit of deception willingly surrender their minds and their wills to believe lies. This leads them deeper and deeper into a place where they are unmercifully held captive to deception. They become completely satisfied with the way things are done and have always been done. The human spirit who is held captive to the influence of the religious spirit just keeps on thinking all is well when it is not. Therefore, The Lord is strongly warning people to be alert and to not relinquish their God-ordained authority against this all-consuming religious spirit. Its wiles are insatiably after people who truly belong to Holy God attempting to get them to give in to its wiles so they don't take a stand against its unauthorized stranglehold and as well do not operate the...*the greater works...* Jesus said they are to do.

However, The Lord is openly disclosing that there are church leaders who recognize the rampant deception of the religious spirit that is operating in the organized church. Therefore, they are not satisfied with the way things are being done that is against Bible Truth, and so they are choosing to come out of the organized church. It is hard for them to do this in front of their children who have been brought up in the church scenario. However, these leaders are following Holy Spirit leadings trusting their children to The Lord believing He will cause them to eventually understand the decisive stand their parents are taking against the actions of the human will aligning with the religious spirit who control the operations of their church.

Parents must honestly and openly tell their children why they freely chose to leave the church they have perhaps attended for years and years. The Lord wants parents to tell their children why they are leaving the organized church and that it is also to OKAY for the children to leave as well. The Lord wants the youth, children, and young adults to know why their parents are leaving the established organized church's traditions, many of which are based on deception and all-out lies perpetuated by the religious spirit who harassed and basically deterred Jesus when He lived on earth.

The Lord is at work in all of those obeying His directions. Therefore, those who wholeheartedly follow the direction of Holy Spirit are being linked together in ways that have never before been considered. Therefore, they are not forsaking the assembling of themselves together during these horrendous times of upheaval to eradicate evil. Closely observe how God is doing this. Then praise and thank Him for working in and through each one of us yet altogether as we obey His directions.

Thank You, Lord Supreme of Heaven and earth, for openly revealing Yourself in Majestic Glory Operations. To You alone be all the Glory and Honor throughout Eternity.

**Satan Rendered Powerless**

I recalled two reality encounters The Lord openly allowed me to observe. The first encounter was on January 19, 1992. The most recent dream was on November 3, 2019. I will begin with the most recent reality encounter that confirms and fulfills the January 19, 1992 reality encounter.

**November 3, 2019**
**DREAM: Satan Stands Impotent Before You**

In a dream, I was alone at home working at my kitchen sink. I was deeply engrossed in what I was doing and was not fully cognizant of the knocking I heard on my pantry door between the kitchen and utility room. I automatically said, "Who is it?" I mechanically went over and opened the door not looking because I was engrossed in what I was doing and so automatically went back to what I was doing at the sink. When I finally did look over at the open pantry door, I explicitly saw a man standing in my pantry. He had not yet walked through the door. He was just standing there. He was totally naked and had no hair on him or his head. He was on crutches, and his right foot was in a blue walking cast. He had no sex organs whatsoever. There was only what looked like skin covering the part of his body where sex organs would be normally. But he looked like a man in appearance. He had a man's haircut and look. He began walking through the door and walking toward me. As I got behind my kitchen island and began heading toward my back door, I cried out, "Get away from me! Stay away from me! Don't you touch me!" With this, I awoke from this dream.

This scenario lingered and remained before me for days. I kept seeing this naked man standing before me over and over. I could not dismiss it. Therefore, I knew it had to have significance and that The Lord wanted me to know something that I did not know. I have been so occupied caring for my husband who had total shoulder replacement I have not had time to pursue The Lord on the meaning of this dream. This morning, I had time to go up to my Prayer Room. I brought this dream before The Lord asking Him to show me what this means.

As I rested in the Presence of The Lord, I knew that what God is giving me to speak and do for Him is causing Satan to stand naked, exposed, crippled, and impotent before me. I knew explicitly that all forms of his evil are being rendered powerless.

Immediately, I recalled the horrible dream I had on **January 19, 1992**, when The Lord began openly speaking to me and giving me revelation.

On this date, I was waking up from an appalling dream I was having that was in such explicit detail that I could not bring myself to even think about it. It was so vivid that I could not shake it from my memory or forget it. I was crying out to God to erase it from my mind. It was so vividly awful that I didn't want to see it or remember it. But it wouldn't go away.

I was crying so hard I scarcely heard the words The Lord was speaking to my heart. I just wanted to forget it, but I couldn't. It kept playing over and over in my mind's eye. As I awoke and got up, I could not get away from this horrible dream. I was greatly disturbed by it. Then I finally realized that God was trying to tell me something. I cried out, "My God and my Lord, what are You telling me?"

The Lord explicitly, plainly, and clearly spoke to me. He said that His Body was allowing themselves to be raped right at the point of fruitfulness and giving birth to what He planted within them. He further revealed that His Body was being raped by their engaging with the lust of the world right at the point of bearing fruit, and this is what was causing them to allow themselves to be raped so they can't bring forth what He implanted within them that is right at the point of fruitfulness.

I cried out asking, "O, Father, what do You want me to do about this?"

I knew intuitively that God, our Father, was going to expose the cause of the rape and show openly that the one who is raping His people is Satan but that he is impotent and powerless and cannot complete or perform the act of raping His people to the point of losing their fruitfulness.

I asked, "How are You going to do this?"

He let me know that this will only be accomplished through affliction that will cause pain and suffering to His people.

I asked, "How does this involve me?"

Instantly, I recalled a previous dream I had had on March 14–15, 1991, where things were at the point of devastation, yet God was using me to *build and plant*. I also recalled His Word to me on October 13, 1983, from Isaiah 14:24–27, 32 about the affliction that He was going to use to drive His people to Himself because they would have no place to flee but to Him, and He would be waiting for them in Zion, a place of refuge where His Presence dwells. He related to me that this pain of affliction is GOOD as it will cause His people to run to Him when they have nowhere else to turn. He stated that after this short affliction comes birth that brings forth fruit from the seed He implanted in His redeemed people so He is seen as Potent and able to perform the ACT of planting seed in the womb of His people that bears fruit. He wants to be seen and known as All-Powerful and able to bring forth the fruit of the womb He implanted within His people that brings forth good fruit that remains.

O, Lord my God, I see this recent dream on November 3, 2019, is confirmation and the fulfillment to the 1992 dream. In truth, Satan is permanently defeated when redeemed people bear Holy fruit for God's Kingdom that remains.

Hallelujah! Your Word endures forever. AMEN.

## Time to Construct and Create

Before going to bed, and seemingly all night long, I was entwined or wrapped around a cylinder-shaped substance that appeared as blue vapor mist. I sensed strongly that The Lord God was wound around me, and we were creating, producing, formulating, generating, constructing, and building. We spun and twirled and rolled flying through space. We were being transported through space. This was so exhilarating and satisfying. I didn't want this to end, and it seemed as if this would never end.

This sensation of spinning and twirling and being transported through space lasted all night long. I wanted this to go on forever. The entire time I was spinning around and around wrapped around this cylinder and blue vapor mist being transported through space, intense Holy Spirit tongue-praying flowed out of me. These strong and forceful tongues never stopped. They just flowed and flowed as if they would never stop. I felt so wrapped in the intensity of His Love and was immensely enjoying this.

I could not shake this visionary yet tangible encounter all day long. Finally, I stopped and wrote this down. When I finished writing this encounter down, these words rose up in me: *construct and create.*

Then I had another dream. I saw a place where people were so joyous and were refurbishing their run-down dwelling places and their meeting places saying to each other with great joy and enthusiasm, "Now we can do this." They were referring to me and expressing how I gave them courage and comprehension to know how to creatively *construct and create* what has been devastated because of what I said to them.

In this dream, I was not there with them doing this restructuring. I wanted to be but was just observing them doing this. It appeared to me that I was excluded in the refurbishing, yet I was with them in all they were doing. I so wanted to be with them and join with them in what they were doing. But I saw all this at a distance.

The Lord revealed to me that He is encouraging me through this dream to know there are those whose lives are being empowered by Holy Spirit to believe the Holy knowledge He is revealing through me to give them so they can *construct and create* new ways to refurbish the old habitations in their lives that have been devastated by evil. *Suddenly*, it became clearly evident to me that this is where things are on earth right now.

The Lord has spoken to me many, many times in various ways over many years that the time would come when He would use me to *build and plant* to restore the devastation caused by evil. Because of all the recent revelation that He took me into, I now have more understanding of His meaning that the time would come for me to *build and plant*. I now have fullness of understanding to know that to *build and plant* means to *construct and create* new ways when everything has been devastated and appears as though it cannot be rebuilt because people are pretty much convinced that the devastation can never be reversed. He has spoken to me for years that He would use me to refurbish new ways in people's lives when it appeared that everything on earth was devastated, and people were saying things on earth could never be restored.

The Lord Almighty is revealing that His Time on earth is here to *construct and create* new ways in people's lives in order to restore and rebuild the foundations that have been ruined and devastated by evil operations. This obvious devastation is causing people to turn to Him. Therefore, I know with certainty that His Time has come to *construct and create* new ways in people's lives in order to restore the foundations of Righteousness that have been destroyed by evil devastation.

Holy Wisdom and Knowledge is being opened by The Lord to His redeemed people so they know how to *construct and create* a fresh environment when everything as they know it to be is devastated. Holy Knowledge and Wisdom is being unleashed to know how to use Visionary Glory to creatively *construct and create* new heavens and new earth. Humankind is Created in God's Image and after His Likeness. Therefore, they innately have creative ability residing within them that gives them the capacity and the capability to *construct and create* what they envision by the Holy desire in their hearts that they release into visible manifestation by the words they speak and the actions they take. This is exactly the Way Supreme God Creatively Created the heavens and the earth.

Creative Glory manifests through people's innate creative ability enabling them to *construct and create* what is needed to rebuild and refurbish right in the midst of the seeming devastation all around them. It doesn't matter to creative people that there is devastation all around them. They are operating by Holy Knowledge and Wisdom by the Creative Glory that is innately Designed within them.

The time has come for people redeemed through Jesus' Blood to step out in Jesus' indwelling (permanently present) *Faith* residing in them to creatively *construct and create* the desire in their hearts that refurbishes their environment as they want it to be. Their enterprises (creativity, innovation, originality) enable them to *con-*

*struct and create* their environment in ways that please them which cause Supreme God's Creative Glory Power to be magnified and exalted so He is seen and known as a Righteous God who Loves His Created people enough to allow them the freedom to *construct and create* their environment in ways they enjoy.

Lord, I appeal to You. Reveal to me in Truth how this will begin. It is one thing to know this but another thing to know how to do this. Are there people with the mindset that this is possible? Do they surmise this is underway? Is their unsettled discontent in the ways things on earth are at this time stirring them up to seek more Knowledge and Wisdom from You? Show me tangibly how to know if this is already underway. I explicitly surrender and yield to You to know what is next in fulfilling Your Word to me that after devastation is the time to *construct and create* to restore what has been devastated by evil. Hasten my knowing, Lord. Help me to understand how this is to be done in fullness. Thank You.

Holy Spirit revelation knowledge opened to me and enlightened my understanding to know that during the unprecedented times on earth when everything on earth and in the heavens is being shaken to remove all forms of evil, God The Almighty Creator of Heaven and earth is exhibiting His unique, Great, and Awesome...*signs, wonders, and miracles*...that outdo Satan's counterfeit signs and wonders. His Holy and Anointed ones ordained by Him are speaking His Word of Authority in Heaven and upon the earth. This Holy interchange between people living on earth, redeemed people in Heaven, and Holy angels in Heaven is releasing an abundant and tangible supply of untainted Power manifestations that provide and restore any needs people on earth have during the unparalleled times when God is pouring out His Holy and Just Wrath to eradicate all evil.

Seeing and experiencing the fulfillment of God's Word causes The Lord's Holy people and angels to cry out to Almighty God of Heaven and earth, "Holy, Holy, Holy, Lord God of Sabaoth, Lord of hosts. You alone are Almighty God of Heaven and earth! Heaven and earth are full of the Glories of Your Majesty. Your Kingdom is an Everlasting Kingdom, and Your dominion endures throughout all generations. You alone are The True and Living God who is worthy to receive All Glory, Honor, and Power and Dominion, for You alone Created All things, and by Your Will, they exist and were Created. Amen and Amen!"

Almighty and benevolent God of all Creation, You are Glorious in all Your Ways. You alone are able to make all Grace, Knowledge, and Wisdom abound to us so that at all times in all ways, we have everything we need to abound in every good work for the Praise of Your Glory. Amen and Amen!

## Unlocking Supernatural Provision

I was randomly reviewing what The Lord has spoken to me concerning His Righteous Kingdom on earth as it pertains to operating in supernatural provision. Luke 12:32, 42 immediately rose up in me:

*Fear not, little flock, for it is your Father's good pleasure to give you the Kingdom.*

*Who then is the faithful and wise steward, whom his master will set over his household, to give them their portion of good at the proper time?*

The Lord is letting it be known on earth and in the heavens that all those who heed His directions are His faithful servants to whom it is His Good Pleasure to give them the Kingdom. Each faithful steward has ownership of all Holy God's possessions. His faithful and obedient servants have all they need at the proper time and so are able to dispense what is needed both physically and spiritually. God has commissioned Holy stewards to dispense food at the proper time to any who have a need. They are set in place over all God's possessions as Righteous stewards who have management and charge over food distribution.

Each one of these Holy stewards may do as they freely choose in meeting the needs of people. Natural circumstances are worsening. It will become evidently clear that supernatural provision needs to operate in full provision to provide people's pressing requirements. Old ways of providing people's needs have passed away. Now is the New Day of supernatural provision so God's Holy Ways are seen on earth. To most, this seems supernatural. To Supreme God, it is His only Way to provide.

Supernatural provision occurs through those who are found faithful by Holy God. These faithful and obedient servants are set by God as His loyal stewards over all His possessions. Shekinah Glory is powerfully removing all forms of evil. Supernatural operations expedited from Visionary Glory release Creative Glory operations to activate and bring into tangible use all the necessities needed for those who belong to God during this time of horrendous and unprecedented upheaval to eradicate evil. It will be known who belongs to God when it is seen that all their necessary needs have been met by Creative Glory operations. God's abundant supernatural provision meets the required needs of His redeemed people living on earth during all the upheaval that is removing all evil. Supernatural provision flows from Visionary Glory.

God's Visionary Glory operates in fullness using these Eternal Rules:

FAITH: in God's Ability to supply
RESPONSE: to hear with focus what God is saying
ACTION: to do what Holy God says to do when He says to do it

Holy God is openly revealing working Knowledge and Wisdom to all who heed His Holy and Just revelation operations. Keep asking Him how and when to do what you innately have the Authority and Power to do through His Presence indwelling you.

## Supernatural Acts Defy World's Logic

In the midst of openly praising and worshipping The Lord, I understood distinctively that all those operating in Visionary Glory are *a sign and a wonder* to show evil principalities, powers, rulers of darkness, and spiritual wickedness in high places that Holy God's Power is superlative and belongs to Him alone, and they cannot touch those who belong to Supreme God in what they are obeying Him to do. His Holy Authority working through His redeemed people is dispensing Justice that dispels darkness and evil and displays His superlative and indispensable Light.

Those who unflinchingly obey Almighty God's Holy directions override the natural system used on earth that these evil powers control by their unholy supernatural operations. Supreme God's Power manifestations defy the world's logic. No longer are things as usual: financial needs being met or supplied through natural means of the world banking system or by those working the religious system by receiving the tithe and offering from people through using God's Word to receive their financial ministry support and as they propose, give to the poor.

No matter how this has worked in the past, it is no longer a viable way to receive necessary provision. Almighty God is closing down the world's financial systems, governmental systems, medical systems, and religious systems who are propagating themselves for self-profit even though they do not believe they are doing this. Deception causes delusion that even takes Holy Scripture and twists it for selfish reasons. Glory operations are being carried out through those who belong to Holy God as they do Creative acts in obedience to His Holy directions. These Glory Fire operations override the world's system of operation. Those operating from Visionary Glory release God's Holy and essential provision to meet people's needs both now and for Infinity.

To God alone be All the Glory, Honor, Power, and Dominion Forever! Amen!

**Kingdom Shift Back to Original Design**

I am coming into increased understanding that all The Lord has openly revealed to me and taught me and sent me to do for Him through the years is currently being confirmed and validated as He promised me. He is clearly showing me how procreation is being done through redeemed people who operate Visionary Glory. In doing this, they are creatively creating the new heavens and new earth that restores and replaces the devastation caused by evil.

This creative restoration brings God's Holy Kingdom back to Original Design that remains for Infinity.

The Lord is presently unveiling hidden revelation that He revealed and spoke to His Holy prophets and had them record at the time He spoke to them which is written in The Holy Bible as we know it today. He has purposely concealed recorded revelation knowledge in The Holy Bible until the time was ripe for this veiled information to be made known for the purpose of fulfilling His Word of Truth. Present world circumstances dictate that the proper time has arrived to uncover these concealed revelations so they are fulfilled as He previously voiced.

Therefore, The Lord is unveiling hidden revelation to those redeemed by Jesus' Holy Blood so they know how to operate Visionary Glory by their innate creative ability He endowed in them before they were born. When they use their innate creative ability by operating Visionary Glory, the new heavens and new earth are created from the desired Holy intent flowing out of their inborn creativity. By doing this, they are utilizing their God-given creativity and Holy Authority to remain in dominion over the part of earth where they choose to reside both now and for Eternity (Revelation 21–22).

God's Original Designed Intent for redeemed humankind to creatively create their own environment is in the process of being completely fulfilled. When redeemed people frame the Holy desired intent in their heart by spoken words of decree and creatively designed actions they receive from Visionary Glory Influence, their holy intention manifests into material form and creates the environment they desire that brings themselves and Holy God pleasure and enjoyment resounding for His Glory throughout Infinity that has no end.

Contemplate Job 22:28 (TAB): *You shall also decide and decree a thing, and it shall be established for you and the light* [of Gods favor] *shall shine upon your ways.*

From their Holy Designed and Creative position in Christ Jesus, redeemed and renewed humankind can construct their desired intent and bring into material manifestation on earth what they frame from the Holy words they speak from Visionary Glory. This brings Supreme God Great Pleasure and Enjoyment to have someone like Himself to fellowship with who creatively creates in the same Way He does. This is His Purpose for Creating humankind in His Image and after His Likeness.

God is Uniquely Creative. He Sovereignly elected to Creatively Design humankind with a free-will to creatively create and manage the Garden, where He placed them, in any way they desired. But human beings used their free-will and listened to the devil's wiles thereby succumbing to his lies that they would be like God in knowing good and evil. God knew evil. However, He never intended for humankind to know evil. The devil betrayed humankind by causing them to believe they could be like God if they knew good and evil. This is true deception at work. The devil is always tricking people into agreeing with him, and this leads them into complying with his selfish will above God's Holy Will, making what he is doing through them by deception appear as their idea, and so he stupidly thinks this excuses him from being detected. The devil even lies to himself to comply with his selfish will above God's Holy *Will* so that it appears as if it was their idea. In this way, he stays under the radar undetected and lets them take the blame for his rebellious evil.

Deception is truth mixed with a lie. God Almighty did not want the people He Created in His Image and Likeness to know the maneuvers of evil so they would be free to use their creative abilities for Good purposes that could never be taken away from them. However, people's disobedience to His Perfect *Will* for them caused sin to enter earth. Their willful rebellion caused them to temporarily lose their ability to creatively create Good things that would remain forever.

Nevertheless, Holy and Living Love came to our rescue. He immediately revealed His Holy Plan to redeem us from Satan's evil (Genesis 2–3). God's Holy and Righteous Goodness drove humankind out of the Garden because if they remained in the Garden in their fallen state of existence, they would remain in this Eternal State that would allow them to Eternally create evil. Thanks be to God who delivers us from ourselves.

For humankind to fulfill God's Original Creative Design in creatively creating their environment as they so choose, a Holy transformation of thinking and speaking must take place in our finite minds so this can occur. We must choose to allow ourselves to transition into Creative Infinity by an act of our free-will. This can be done when Father, Son, and Holy Spirit's essential and actual abiding Presence resides in us. His abiding Presence dwelling in us transforms our thinking so we think and act as He does. As we submit to our Righteous Godhead: Father, Son, and Holy Spirit, His Infinite Creative Ability Intent continuously operates in us for good.

Even before we were born, God had a plan for our lives. He intentionally Designed within us our creative ability to transform our environment into what we creatively construct from our Holy desire by the words we speak. As we continually allow the fullness of Supreme God's Presence indwelling us to transform our thinking, we are

Creative Infinity activated and realized. This creative ability remains in redeemed people when they graduate to Heaven and continues to operate through them for Eternity. This creative ability also exists within all living beings Supreme God Created and endorsed with His Stamp of approval.

Creative God Originally Designed for the entire company or assembly of beings in Heaven along with humankind on earth to flow together with Him in creatively creating a beautifully and creatively designed environment for all of us to enjoy together for Infinity. Each God-Created Holy being is uniquely fashioned so that our creative abilities flow together to fulfill God's Predetermined Plan for His Creations to exist together in perfect harmony. Therefore, His intended purpose is for all His Created beings to work together as one united and Holy Plan according to their uniquely and Creatively Designed aptitude.

**Prayer:**
In Jesus' Name, I call forth a shift back to Original Kingdom Living. According to Hebrews 12:22-24, I call out to heavenly Jerusalem, the city of God in Heaven, the cloud of witnesses in Heaven—innumerable company of angels, the general assembly and church of the firstborn, to God the Judge of all, to the spirits of just men made perfect, to Jesus the Mediator of the new covenant, and to the blood of sprinkling that speaks better things to come and join in accomplishing together our Holy Assignments from Supreme God. I entreat you to come to us and exchange Holy facts with us to establish Kingdom Living back to its Original form so that Holy God's Planned Intention for the heavens and earth to cooperate together in one complete and Holy Circle of Life is completed for Infinity. Amen!

I truly and deeply and innately perceive and therefore wholeheartedly believe by Holy Spirit of Supreme God abiding in me that there are those of you who have had or are having dream or vision encounters where you are creatively creating or designing something for good *that you know, that you know, that you know* is real. In fact, it is so real that to you, it is already a done deal. Yet you stay quiet about this hesitating to share this with anyone, but you feel you are about to burst if you don't release this creative intent so deeply ingrained within you.

I lovingly implore you not to hide this any longer. Instead, go forward in some way no matter how small or insignificant these dreams and visions may seem to you. Move forward with what is burning in your heart to do or to share with others concerning your creative vision or dream. **Without a vision, the people perish**. You may have the very vision that will keep people from perishing and that will enhance them to come into the fullness of their God-given creativeness. We all need each other to enhance our lives and fulfill the God-Created destiny He Creatively Created in us that is to be achieved for Infinity.

**Imagination is the seed of creativity.**

What you creatively imagine grows and blossoms into fruit that brings fruitfulness to your God-given creative intent. You have the ability to bring this creative imagination into actual being by the words you speak and the actions you take. Keep reading and rereading this book to prepare yourself to fulfill your creative destiny.

When you step out and do what is in your heart to do and then meet head-on what you suppose is failure, just remember it is not failure. It just shows you that there is still more to be learned for your creative design to be achieved. Always learn from supposed mistakes. No mistake is a mistake. Mistakes are just training opportunities. Keep pursuing. Each step you take and each endeavor you explore is leading you to attain your innate creative design that you clearly know will help others. Keep on seeking and asking all kinds of questions to God and to people. No question is a dumb question. It proves that you are seeking Wisdom to know how to continue fulfilling your God-ordained Creative Destiny.

The Lord's Seven Spirits have eyes full of Wisdom and Knowledge. Wisdom is empowered by Prudence who imparts Knowledge into all the Seven Spirits who carry you into the situations on earth to accomplish Holy God's preordained Plan. God's time is here for those He Created in His Image and Likeness to operate in supernatural ways that are opposite of the world's ways. God's Holy Ways bring righteous gain for the Holy Purpose of reconciling Heaven and earth back into His Originally Designed Intent.

It must be made known explicitly that God's Creative Plan for Heaven and earth to flow as One Complete Circle of Life has been hijacked by Satan. He selfishly perverted his Creative ability endowed in him by His Creator. Satan used his God-Fashioned creative abilities for his own selfish gain. He wrongly set out to make a name for himself by persuading others to join in with his deplorable plans to build a false kingdom of his own making.

**Satan's evil creativity destroys. Supreme God's Holy Creative Ability expands and establishes GOOD outcomes for His Creations.**

Through redeemed humankind creatively designing and procreating their environment by Holy means, God

Almighty is reversing the evil intent in the hearts and minds of mankind put there by Satan in his attempt to control them for his own selfish purposes of building his own evil empire.

Supreme God Originally Designed humankind to combine their creative efforts to create an environment they desired to inhabit for their social enjoyment. The following Biblical account reveals the creative capacity that innately resides within each human being.

*Now the whole earth had one language and one speech. And it came to pass, as they journeyed from the east, that they found a plain in the land of Shinar, and they dwelt there. Then they said to one another. "**Come, let us** make bricks and bake them thoroughly." They had brick for stone, and they had asphalt for mortar. And they said, "**Come, let us** build ourselves a city, and a tower whose top is in the heavens; let us **make a name for ourselves**, lest we be scattered abroad over the face of the whole earth."*

*But The Lord came down to see the city and the tower which the sons of men had built. And **The Lord said, "Indeed, the people are one and they all have one language, and this is only the beginning of what they will do; now nothing they have imagined will be impossible for them.** Come let Us go down there and confuse their language, that they may not understand one another's speech."*

*So The Lord scattered them abroad from there over the face of all the earth, and they ceased building the city. Therefore, the name of it was called Babel—because there The Lord confused the language of all the earth; and from there The Lord scattered them abroad over the face of all the earth.* (Genesis 11:1-9)

People on earth at that time were attempting to use their innately God-created abilities to build and create a city for themselves to enjoy. However, Satan thwarted their good intentions of creatively creating a city for themselves through their innate creativity by duping them by evil deception and lies based on self-importance that caused them to selfishly want to stay in one place and not spread out into all the world. Holy God had bigger plans for the whole world, not just for one region on earth.

At this time on earth, Holy God is intervening within corrupted history and making Himself known as Supreme God. He is releasing Holy Revelation Knowledge and Wisdom as to how He intends to restore back to Original Design what He Creatively Created for humankind to achieve.

Through what is written in this book and through what others as well are writing from what The Lord is revealing to them, The Lord is openly revealing how He is fulfilling His Holy Originally Designed Plan for humankind and Heavenly beings to unitedly work together in complete harmony, peace, and creativity in order to creatively create the environment they desire to inhabit for Infinity.

**Overseers in Charge of Cities**

The Lord poured out to me knowledge that was unknown to me which opened my understanding of things I do not know that I need to know as I asked Him to do. He poured into me a download of Truth from His Holy Word, The Bible, as recorded in Matthew 8:5-11, Luke 7:1-9, Luke

19:11–27, Jeremiah 3:17, Revelation 21:2–7, 22:1–6. Then He went beyond human understanding by mystically revealing Himself in the way He and His Righteous Kingdom truly exists.

Jesus' parable in Matthew 8:5–11 reveals a centurion who understood authority and how to wisely use his authority for the good of his servants. Jesus was astounded that this centurion so rightly understood Kingdom Authority. Seeing the faith and action of this centurion so blessed Jesus because most in Israel, to whom He was sent, did not understand Kingdom Authority because they were so full of themselves.

In Luke 19:11–27, Jesus told this parable to His disciples because they supposed that the Kingdom of God was to appear immediately. Therefore, Jesus related to His disciples that there was a nobleman who went into a distant country to obtain for himself a kingdom, but before he left, he called ten of his servants and gave them money and told them to go and trade and bring him an increase on his investment by investing what he gave them until he returned. The nobleman was expecting a return on his investment. There were those who decided that they didn't want this nobleman to reign over them when he became king. So they sent a delegation after him telling him they did not want him to rule over them when he received his kingdom. When the nobleman did return having received the kingdom, he commanded these servants to give him an account of what they gained in trading with the monetary investment he entrusted to them. Some were good stewards of what was entrusted to them because they multiplied what they were given and received a return on his investment to give him. The nobleman rewarded them according to the return on their investment. Then he gave them authority to rule over cities in his kingdom. Some would rule over ten cities, some over five cities. Those who did not want the nobleman to rule over them were brought before him to give an account of what he monetarily entrusted to them, and those who had nothing to give him in return were slain before him for not giving him a return on his investment he entrusted to them.

This story or parable Jesus told has Eternal impact and significance. Jesus is talking about the Kingdom of Righteousness that His Father gave Him to Rule. He is Truthfully stating that those presently living on earth who invest in His Holy Kingdom are setting themselves up to receive Eternal rewards that include ruling over cities for Infinity.

In Jeremiah 3:17, The Lord gave Jeremiah a message of hope to give to His people:

*Jerusalem shall be called The Throne of The Lord, and all the nations shall be gathered to it, to the name and presence of the Lord in Jerusalem and they shall no more stubbornly follow the dictates of their own evil hearts.*

I saw in Revelation 21 and 22 a new heaven and a new earth and a Holy city where nothing unclean or evil shall ever enter. Only those whose names are written in the Lamb's Book of Life will be allowed to enter and creatively inhabit this city for Infinity.

The Lord unveiled Holy revelation of Himself that granted me Holy Insight as to how His Rule of Righteousness is being carried out in the new heavens and new earth through those He is rewarding for their faithfulness in bringing Him an investment on what He entrusted to them while they lived on earth.

The Lord unveiled distinct revelation to know that there is an overseer appointed and set by God to oversee a city on the new earth. An overseer can be in charge of more than one city. The overseer assigned by God for each city can come to the Court in Heaven and make an appeal to have the Book for their city opened to them. When the overseer is granted their request, they are entrusted with the information that is written in the Book for their city, and they present it to the people in the city they oversee.

The person appointed by God to oversee their city is the one who goes back and forth from Heaven to earth to make an appeal before Heaven's Court to have the Book for their city opened for them to look into and get the assignments written in the Book for their city. This is how the people on the new earth discover their city's intended assignment. Each redeemed and resurrected person receives their assignments from the Court in Heaven from what is written in their Book that is to be creatively used on earth or in the heavens. All assignments come from the Court in Heaven. This goes on for Eternity.

The overseer for each city in the new earth also has legal access to each person's Book in Heaven's Court that reveals their unique assignment for their city that can be used in the city where they reside. Each person can come to the overseer of the city where they live asking to know what is written in their Book in Heaven's Court. Their personal inquiry releases the overseer to go ahead and access the Book that contains their assignment and relate it to them. The overseer comes into agreement with their Holy creative assignment and releases this person to freely use their God-given creative ability and creative talents in conjunction with all the others in their city who are using their unique creative abilities for the benefit of the whole community that enhances the welfare of their city.

Each person brings their assignment into existence in their city from whatever they desire and frame by their Holy words of passionate intent. This Holy design is accomplished when each person speaks creative words and does actions proceeding from the Holy intent in their hearts. Each person operates from their own designed order as they were endowed by their Creator. These collective desires coincide and develop the creative purpose for their city for the enjoyment of the entire city and anyone who comes to see and enjoy their city.

The overseer and the people work together in harmony because there is no longer jealousy or opposition from human spirits tainted by Satan's evil. The human spirit sanctified by Jesus' Blood truly wants to put their part with another's part so all flow together and fulfill the Holy intended design for their city that brings collective enjoyment for all.

Holy and Supreme God alone has established a Holy Order that is to be followed for the welfare of Heaven and earth flowing together as One Complete Holy Operation. Actually, this is how it is meant to be on earth at this time. However, this is not being fully understood or carried out in Righteousness with an Eternal view because evil still reigns in most situations.

Ponder that at this time on earth, each city, state, region, and country has a distinct flavor or unique creativity and design as to how each person in the city or area adds their talent or creative gift to make their city a unique setting that draws people from other cities, regions, and countries to come and enjoy their city and region and country and its surroundings. Cities on earth at this time put out advertisements inviting people to come to their city and enjoy and experience their uniqueness. However, because evil reigns on earth at this time, jealousy is causing wrongly motivated competition with each city trying to outdo the other for selfish reasons.

When evil is fully removed, no one is jealous or tries to overthrow or overtake another's position of Authority. No longer are other people's possessions stolen nor is their creativity disrupted by evil intent. People are free to come and go as they please to each other's cities and stay and enjoy the people and their environment as long as they desire. Every single person enjoys each other and blesses each other's uniqueness and creativity by saying, "Come and see!" From this invitation, each person freely decides when they want to go and see another city and how long they want to stay. This invitation goes on for Eternity.

There are also those who especially desire to explore the new heavens. Those who desire to explore and creatively create in the new heavens can come before the Court in Heaven making an appeal for the Book to be opened to them that has the Blueprint that can be accomplished in the new heavens.

When they appeal to the Court of Heaven to have the exact Book opened that reveals what can be creatively created in the new heavens, the Book will be opened to them according to what is written in this Book that is in line with their unique creative design as endowed in them by their Creator.

When this Book in the Court of Heaven is legally opened to them, they recognize from what is written in this Book how to creatively design the new heavens according to their desired Holy intent. From this Holy Knowledge, they formulate and build their desired Holy intent in the new heavens by speaking into existence what they construct by their Holy words.

Those who innately desire to creatively create in the new heavens form their Holy desired intent by speaking from the Substance of Life abiding in the Godhead: Father, Jesus, Holy Spirit what they desire to see accomplished in the new heavens that aligns with what is recorded in the Book pertaining to the new heavens. From the desired Holy intent that is innately Designed within them, they creatively create what they desire by speaking it into existence. What they creatively create in the new heavens remains and is useful for Eternity.

Whoa! What a Glorious existence this is, Lord! Hallelujah! AMEN!

Consider as well that redeemed people *can* live in Peace, Joy, and Harmony and perfect Rest right now in time on earth even in the midst of chaos and upheaval because Almighty God's work of redemption was finished when Jesus declared on the Cross, ...*It is finished!*...and then committed His Spirit into His Father's keeping.

Jesus willingly agreed to be His Father's Living Sacrifice to pay for the sins of mankind who rebelled against their Creator when they followed Satan's deceptive evil. Jesus' Holy Sacrifice in dying on the cross to take away the sin of the world and then rising from the dead in Resurrection Power redeems humankind from all Satan's evil works and ways (1 John 3:8). Therefore, right now during God's ordained time frame on earth, redeemed saints who accept Jesus' Salvation from evil and live as though they do are truly and fully living in Eternity by living daily in Jesus' provision of Eternal Ways of Rest, Harmony, Love, Peace, and Joy. This way of Life exists no matter where redeemed people reside in time on earth or in their Heavenly abode. There is only One Circle of Life that exists on earth and in Heaven.

By Faith in God's Ability to complete His *Will* for Heaven and earth, people living in time on earth can live in the Eternal Ways of Eternity that never ends. When we understand Infinity, we know that we can presently live in Eternal Rest, Harmony, Love, Peace, and Joy in the Eternity of no time. As we live on earth in Eternal Ways by Holy God's provision, Satan has no advantage over us. Therefore, whether we exist on earth in time, which is actually a part of Infinity, or continue our existence in Heaven, we live Eternally with Jesus (Ephesians 2:1–7).

The Lord had me write this book, *Creative Living from Original Design*, for those of you who know there is so much more than what you are presently experiencing in your circumstances. For you who know this, you can freely choose to break out and break forth into Creative motion to fulfill whatever Holy God has innately implanted within you to obtain for Infinity. **Go for it!** Don't allow yourself to be dissuaded by unholy and ungodly influences.

Supreme God is for you. So who can be against you? No one, unless you allow them to persuade you differently than from what Holy God says to you as recorded in His Holy Word, The Bible.

As Romans 8:31 states:
*If God is for us who can be against us? He who did not spare His own Son but gave Him up for us all, will He not also give us all things with Him?*

God says in His Word many times: *I will never leave you nor forsake you.*

He also states in Hebrews 13:6, 8:
*The Lord is my helper; I will not fear. What can man do to me? Jesus Christ the same yesterday, today, and forever!*

*Therefore, we can say what David said,*

*The Lord is always with me. I will not be shaken for He is right beside me. The Lord shows me the way of Life. He fills me with the joy of His Presence.* (Acts 2:25-28)

At this time on earth, The Lord God of Heaven and earth is openly revealing Himself in Holy celestial Ways that are far above self-thinking ways. Are you one who truly desires to know Him in celestial ways? When you seek Holy God's Heart to know Him in relationship, you will find Him. He knows and hears your heart's intent and comes to you in Ways that are unique to the way He Originally Designed you to relate to Him.

Holy God can be found by you. **If** you diligently and wholeheartedly seek The Lord God, your Creator, and keep on seeking Him, you will find Him. The Lord God says in Isaiah 45 that if He couldn't be found, He wouldn't say that He could be found:

*For The Lord is God. He created the heavens and the earth. He put everything in place. He made world to be lived in, not to be a place of empty chaos. I am The Lord and there is no other. I publicly proclaim bold promises. I do not whisper obscurities in some dark corner. I would not have told the people of Israel to seek Me, if I could be found. I, The Lord, speak only what is true and declare only what is right.* (Isaiah 45:18–19 New Living Translation)

*The Lord is waiting on you to come to Him so He can show you His Love and Compassion. The Lord is a faithful God. He is Gracious to you if you ask Him for help. He surely responds to the sound of your cries.* (Isaiah 30:18–19 New Living Translation)

How do you choose to devote and occupy your Life Holy God innately Created in you to fulfill before you were born on earth? Only you can answer this. Your free-will choices determine the way you can enjoy life on earth at this time and also where you occupy Eternal Living that goes on forever and ever with no end. Choose wisely!

How you choose to creatively live from Original Design is your Infinite Destiny!

I, Betsy, want it to be known in the writing of this book that what Jesus and Paul declared as written in The Holy Bible is most certainly true for me as well:

*My teaching is not My own, but His who sent Me. If any man's will is to do His will, he shall know whether the teaching is from God or whether I am speaking on My own authority.*

*He who speaks on his own authority seeks his own glory, but He who seeks the Glory of Him who sent him is true, and in him there is no falsehood.* (John 7:16–18)

*I do nothing on My own authority but speak what the Father taught Me. He sent Me. He who sent Me is with Me. I always do what is pleasing to Him.* (John 8:28b–29)

*I have not come of my own accord; He who sent Me is true, and I know Him, for I come from Him, and He sent Me.* (John 8:42)

*If I tell you the Truth, why do you not believe Me? He who is of God hears the words of God; the reason you do not hear them is that you are not of God.* (John 8:46–47)

*I do not come to you with excellence of speech or persuasive words of human wisdom, but in demonstration of The Spirit and of Power that your faith is not in the wisdom of men, but in the Power of God.* (1 Corinthians 2:4–5)

*I am not sufficient of myself to claim that anything comes from me; my sufficiency is from God, who has qualified me to be a minister of a new covenant written in me by The Spirit of god who gives life.* (2 Corinthians 3:5-6)

*I have this ministry by the mercy of God... I do not preach about myself, but I preach Jesus Christ as Lord, with myself as a servant for Jesus' sake. For God said, 'Let light shine out of darkness,' who has shone in our hearts to give the light of the knowledge of the glory of God in the face of Christ.*

*I have this treasure in an earthen vessel to show that the transcendent power belongs to God and not me.* (2 Corinthians 4:1, 5-7)

I want to give all Glory, thanksgiving and deference to Supreme and Living God for exhibiting His Creative Personality to me in so many manners and ways to indelibly inscribe on my heart and in my spirit how to transcribe all the ways He displays His many-sided facets of never-ending Beauty and Creativity that can be discovered for Infinity. Without His abiding Presence we can do nothing.

## About the Author

Before Betsy was born, Holy and Supreme God of all Creation Sovereignly Designed her to Creatively know Him. Betsy's lifelong interactive training by Living God enables her to clearly make Him known as Creative God in the way He desires to be known.

Betsy Fritcha is also the author of the globally acclaimed books, *Apocalypse: Here and Now! Are you Ready?* She as well has authored *Shekinah Glory Reveals Wisdom: The Voice of The Lord Speaks*; *Israel's Glory Unveiled*; and *Infinite Destiny: Truth and Wisdom*, which depict Betsy's personal lifetime celestial interactive journeys with Creative and Holy God. All of Betsy's books are available on Amazon, Barnes & Noble, and Betsy's website: www.spiritofgodvoice.com, as well as other venues.

Contact Betsy at AnointedLife1@Frontier.com